QUANGOs AND LOCAL GOVERNMENT
A Changing World

HOWARD DAVIS

FRANK CASS
LONDON • PORTLAND, OR

First published in 1996 in Great Britain by
FRANK CASS AND COMPANY LIMITED
Newbury House, 900 Eastern Avenue, London IG2 7HH, England

and in the United States of America by
FRANK CASS
c/o International Specialized Book Services, Inc.
5804 N.E. Hassalo Street, Portland, Oregon 97213-3644

Copyright © 1996 Frank Cass & Co. Ltd

British Library Cataloguing in Publication Data

QUANGOs and local government:
    a changing world
    1.Local government - Great Britain
    I.Davis, Howard, 1953-
    352'.041

ISBN 0 7146 4735 7 (cloth)
ISBN 0 7146 4324 6 (paper)

Library of Congress Cataloging-in-Publication Data

QUANGOs and local government: a changing world
        p. cm.
    "This group of studies first appeared in a Special Issue of Local
Government Studies, Vol. 22, No. 2 (Summer 1996)."
        ISBN 0-7146-4735-7 (cloth)
        1. Local government--Great Britain.   2. Administrative agencies-
    -Great Britain.   3. Executive advisory bodies--Great Britain.
    I. Davis, Howard.
    JS3111.C47 1996
    320.8'5'0941--dc20   96-14813
                                                    CIP

This group of studies first appeared in a Special Issue of *Local Government Studies*, Vol.22, No.2 (Summer 1995), [QUANGOs and Local Government: A Changing World].

Contents

QUANGOs and Local Government:
A Changing World   Howard Davis   1

Understanding the New Magistracy: Chris Skelcher
A Study of Characteristics and Attitudes   and Howard Davis   8

Business as Usual? The New Police Authorities
and the Police and Magistrates' Courts Act   Barry Loveday   22

Independence in Further Education: Managing
the Change Process   Jean C. Easton   40

Public Accountability in Today's Health Service   Guy B.J. Daly   52

The Indirectly Elected World of Local Government   Steve Leach   64

Lessons from Local Government in Northern
Ireland   Michael Connolly   77

'Working the Network': Local Authority Strategies
in the Reticulated Local State   David Prior   92

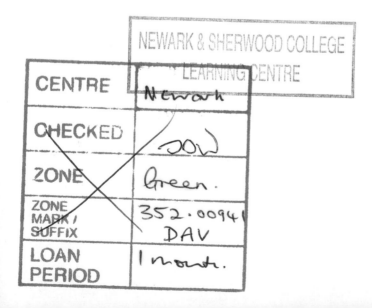

QUANGOs and Local Government: A Changing World

HOWARD DAVIS

THE GROWTH OF GOVERNMENT BY APPOINTMENT

Recent years have seen a major transformation in the way that local communities are governed. There has been a growth of 'government by appointment'.[1] It has, of course, never been the case that local authorities have exercised all governmental powers in any particular locality. Others have always been involved but, in the past, local authorities confidently saw themselves as the rightful and undisputed leaders of their communities. Now their position is under challenge as they find themselves sharing the local 'turf' with a whole range of bodies also exercising governmental powers at the local level. Figure 1 outlines the growth of government by appointment.

FIGURE 1
THE GROWTH OF GOVERNMENT BY APPOINTMENT

- Local authority representatives removed from District Health Authorities (DHAs) and from Family Health Service Authorities (FHSAs).
- Appointed boards set up to run the newly created Health Service Trusts.
- Training and Enterprise Councils created to exercise training and development functions at local level, many of which were once exercised by local authorities.
- Self-appointing boards of governors took over responsibility from local authorities for polytechnics, further education colleges and sixth form colleges. They are now subject to the requirements of funding councils, themselves nationally appointed bodies.
- Schools encouraged to opt out of local authority control and become grant-maintained schools, which are also financed by new funding councils appointed nationally.
- Housing Action Trusts and Urban Development Corporations appointed to take over local authority responsibilities in selected small areas.
- Proposals announced to remove the responsibilities of local authorities for policing matters and transfer them to newly appointed police authorities. (Although the original proposals were later modified, the link with local government has been significantly weakened.)

Source: Adapted from J. Stewart and H. Davis, 'A New Agenda for Local Governance', *Public Money and Management*, Oct.–Dec. 1994, p.29.

Howard Davis, The University of Birmingham

FIGURE 2
COUNCILLORS AND APPOINTEES IN THE WEST MIDLANDS:
THE CHANGING BALANCE

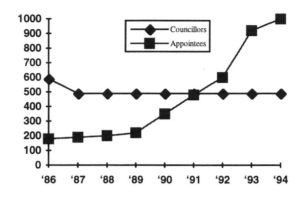

Source: H. Davis (ed.), *QUANGOs and Local Government: Issues and Responses* (Inlogov, 1995), p.5.

The number of members of appointed and self-appointed bodies who, following Morris,[2] have become known as the 'new magistracy', now greatly exceeds the number of elected local councillors. By way of example, an analysis of the situation in the West Midlands metropolitan county shows that the number of 'new magistrates' is now twice the number of councillors in that area (see Figure 2).

This volume is concerned with developing understanding of the new and changing world of local governance. It is, of necessity, selective in its coverage. The topics covered do, however, give a flavour of the changes that have been taking place and include joint working, managing a change of status, partnerships and networks.

BLURRED BOUNDARIES: A CAUSE FOR CONCERN?

There is now an appointed world of local governance sitting alongside elected local government. Many appointed bodies (popularly known as QUANGOs) are seen, from the local government perspective, as 'domain intruders'[3] and are often viewed with resentment and suspicion. Certainly organisational roles and boundaries have become more blurred and confused. This blurring and confusion is added to by some of the new organisational titles. Training and Enterprise Councils are not councils in the sense that that term is normally understood, but companies limited by guarantee. Housing Action Trusts and Education Associations are both government-appointed bodies, rather than the independent bodies that their titles imply.

Some may question whether such issues matter, but acceptance of different definitions can lead to acceptance of different principles or standards. Some in the housing associations, for instance, have sought to distance themselves from wider debates about standards of governance for public services.[4] Riseborough, however, has referred to the 'doubtful voluntary status' of housing associations saying that they 'have been colonised by the state and in their case the boundaries between public, private and voluntary have not so much been blurred as elided'.[5]

The Nolan Committee on Standards in Public Life has implicitly joined this debate by extending its investigations to include what it terms 'local public spending bodies', 'By this we mean 'not for profit' bodies which are neither fully elected nor appointed by ministers, but which provide public services, often delivered at local level which are wholly or largely publicly funded'.[6] Lord Nolan himself comments that,

> We are charged with examining key areas of public life and, if necessary, making recommendations designed to ensure that the highest standards are maintained, and are seen to be maintained ... we are looking at local public spending bodies ... because the services which they provide are very important to us all. They have been subject to great change in recent years. We need to be sure that in seeking improvements in service we have not put at risk those values and standards which are the cornerstone of public life.[7]

The key principles – the seven principles of public life – were earlier set out by the Committee in its first report and are reproduced here as Figure 3.

FRAGMENTATION AND ACCOUNTABILITY

'Holders of public office' is a key phrase used by Nolan and defining sectoral boundaries is therefore a potentially significant issue if principles such as those below are to apply – which surely they must. There can be no justifiable reason for applying different standards to different public services simply because the bodies which provide them are constituted in different forms. It is a matter of considerable regret that, in the absence of direct electoral accountability, many of the other bodies now sharing territory with local government have a less rigorous framework of accountability.[8]

FIGURE 3
THE SEVEN PRINCIPLES OF PUBLIC LIFE

Selflessness
Holders of public office should take decisions solely in terms of the public interest. They should not do so in order to gain financial or other material benefits for themselves, their family, or their friends.

Integrity
Holders of public office should not place themselves under any financial or other obligation to outside individuals or organisations that might influence them in the performance of their official duties.

Objectivity
In carrying out public business, including making public appointments, awarding contracts, or recommending individuals for rewards and benefits, holders of public office should make choices on merit.

Accountability
Holders of public office are accountable for their decisions and actions to the public and must submit themselves to whatever scrutiny is appropriate to their office.

Openness
Holders of public office should be as open as possible about all the decisions and actions that they take. They should give reasons for their decisions and restrict information only when the wider public interest clearly demands.

Honesty
Holders of public office have a duty to declare any private interests relating to their public duties and to take steps to resolve any conflicts arising in a way that protects the public interest.

Leadership
Holders of public office should promote and support these principles by leadership and example.

Source: Committee on Standards in Public Life (the Nolan Committee), First Report, Cmnd 2850-I (HMSO, 1995), p.14.

The increased importance and number of appointed bodies exercising governmental powers locally has led to a growing fragmentation of community governance. It is a development that has a profound significance. As we have noted in an earlier publication,

The fragmentation of the government of cities, towns and rural areas between different organizations and institutions is reducing the capacity of the system to deal with issues that require different functions or institutions to work together. Yet many of the emerging issues in our society require just such a capacity for integration ... Above all, many towns and cities face deep transformations. Their economic base has been destroyed, creating in that change deep social problems. They seek a new industrial and service base, and to establish a new economic and social role. Such changes cannot be brought about by any one organization. Action by many individuals and organizations – in both the public and private sectors – is required. But directions need to be set out; co-operation is required in seeking out and following those directions. That is not easily achieved in a fragmented system of government.[9]

Governmental systems need a capacity for integration. In a fragmented system different policy agendas have to be brought together and new forms of relationship must be built, yet 'the capacity of local government to provide that direction through civic leadership is reduced'.[10]

Effective networks, partnerships and joint arrangements can be built, as some of the contributions to this volume demonstrate, yet the vexed question of accountability remains. Arrangements for improved stewardship and managerial accountability may be put into place. These are surely to be welcomed, but the issue of how to hold decision makers *to account* remains largely unresolved.

Current arrangements for local government elections may well have their faults. Nevertheless, councillors are, in principle, subject to removal through this process and, as such, are imbued with a legitimacy that board members of appointed and self-appointed bodies do not enjoy. Local democratic accountability is a key issue in the emerging system of local governance and it is something that local authorities can 'bring to the table' in their discussions and negotiations with other bodies at the local level.

DEVELOPING UNDERSTANDING

This volume seeks to develop understanding of the changing world of local governance and thus contribute to wider debates. Chris Skelcher and Howard Davis draw on their recent Rowntree-funded research on the membership of local appointed bodies to explore the world of local appointed members, their characteristics and attitudes, and contrast this with survey information about local councillors. This is followed by a contribution from Barry Loveday on the new free-standing police authorities and on the selection of the new 'independent' members of these authorities. He concludes that,

It might yet be a source of some irony if the continuing centralising pressure from the Home Office generated alliances between police and police authorities which rejected the more overt forms of interference in operational policing which increasingly characterise current Home Office policy.

Jean Easton gives a detailed account of how further education colleges in Birmingham and Solihull have been managing the change to independent status. In the process of change relationships were said to be uneasy but the new networks were seen to be developing a new confidence and maturity. She feels, however, that there is a danger that the pursuit of 'business achievement' could take priority over community values. Guy Daly tackles the issue of accountability for local health services, strongly challenging current arrangements. His view is that 'tinkering with the system is no longer a credible response'. 'The inescapable conclusion must be that there can be no effective substitute for the local ballot box.'

The next contribution, from Steve Leach, addresses a frequently overlooked aspect of the debate about appointed bodies – the joint boards and joint committees responsible for providing certain local services in some parts of the country. He notes that they occupy an 'interesting intermediate position' between 'the direct accountability of local authorities and the opaque accountability processes of appointed bodies'. Michael Connolly then sets out the Northern Irish experience. One of the reasons for looking at Northern Ireland is that 'the logical outcome of the model of reduced local government' already exists there. Connolly concludes that, 'Even when local government is denuded of other roles, councillors seek to play a political role. Indeed the evidence from Northern Ireland suggests that the political role expands when other roles are eliminated'.

Finally, David Prior focuses on emerging local governance networks and the ability of local authorities to 'work' those networks, together with the implications for their own organisational structures. He notes that 'working within the new networks of local governance has become increasingly significant for local authorities' but comments that it does

> pose a major challenge for local authorities to the extent that it implies a new and different approach to their own internal policy processes. Whether local authorities can respond by transforming their internal roles and relationships to support their changing role in the external environment may be a critical factor in determining whether they can consolidate and enhance their position as the leaders of local networks or whether they will be relegated to a role of camp followers.

CONCLUDING REMARKS

Changes made to the structure and organisation of local services have had a major impact on local government and on the governance of each and every community. The impact of these changes will continue to be felt for many years to come – whoever is in government. Clarke and Stewart comment,

> At one level, community governance just happens. That is to say, relevant and related organisations and agencies will find ways of interacting and working with one another as appropriate. In another way, though, active encouragement and formality is needed ... Ways need to be found of bringing into both the debate and action the diverse communities of interest who would otherwise be excluded.[11]

These are surely key messages for all involved with local public services – however defined.

NOTES

I am grateful to my colleague Chris Skelcher for commenting on drafts of this article.

1. H. Davis and J. Stewart, *The Growth of Government by Appointment* (Local Government Management Board, 1993).
2. R. Morris, *Central and Local Control After the Education Reform Act 1988* (Longman, 1990).
3. S. Leach, M. Clarke, A. Campbell, H. Davis and S. Rogers, *Minimising Fragmentation: Managing Services, Leading Communities* (Local Government Management Board, 1996).
4. P. Cole, 'Behind that QUANGOs Tag', *HA Weekly*, 4 Nov. 1994, pp.12–15.
5. M. Riseborough, 'Housing Associations: Voluntary, Charity or Non-Profit Bodies?', paper presented to NCVO Voluntary Sector Conference, London, 1995
6. Committee on Standards in Public Life (the Nolan Committee), *Local Public Spending Bodies: Issues and Questions* (HMSO, 1995), para.2.
7. Ibid., foreword by the Rt Hon Lord Nolan.
8. H. Davis and J. Stewart, op. cit.
9. J. Stewart and H. Davis, op. cit., p.30.
10. Ibid.
11. M. Clarke and J. Stewart, *District Councils and Community Governance* (Association of District Councils, 1995), p.13.

Understanding the New Magistracy: A Study of Characteristics and Attitudes

CHRIS SKELCHER and HOWARD DAVIS

The motivation, characteristics and political behaviour of local councillors have been matters for debate since the beginnings of the British system of local government. Social reformers in the early part of this century commented on the need for good governance at the local level and for councillors who approached the task with commitment and dedication. In the post-war years the Maud and Widdicombe Reports have again dealt with questions of councillor competence and background, and more recently the review of the internal management of local authorities has explored proposals which – in a UK context – appear quite radical. Yet alongside the local government system there operate another set of bodies which make governmental decisions affecting local communities. These local QUANGOs have boards of individuals who in most cases are appointed by a central government minister, another agency or the existing board members themselves. The number of local QUANGOs has increased markedly in recent years, both in terms of their numbers and the areas of public policy over which they operate.[1] However, their constitution and mode of operation, when compared with that of local government, makes them more remote from local political processes and the communities they serve. Their boards' relative closure to public view and scrutiny, combined with an absence of readily available public information and academic research, has resulted in a dearth of information about these 'new magistrates'.[2] Unlike councillors, their motivation, characteristics and 'political' behaviour has seldom been subject to investigation.

This article explores the world of local appointed members. It reports data gathered in a major survey of eight types of local executive QUANGO in England (Table 1).[3] During 1994 postal questionnaires were sent to the chair of the board in a sample of bodies in each of the eight sectors, with a request that they be circulated to all non-executive (that is, appointed) members. The sample size varied according to the number of bodies in each of the eight classes of QUANGO. Semi-structured interviews were also conducted with a small number of appointed members and senior managers

Chris Skelcher and Howard Davis, The University of Birmingham

TABLE 1
THE CHARACTERISTICS OF LOCAL QUANGOS IN THE STUDY

Type of Body	No. in England[a]	Geographical Coverage	Date Established	Status
City Challenge	31	Partial; focus on specific localities within urban areas	In two phases from 1992; expected life of 5 years	Usually company limited by guarantee created by local authority and other partners; appoints own board
Urban Development Corporations	12	Partial; focus on special localities	In four phases from 1981; expected life of 5-15 years	Non-Departmental Public Body appointed by Secretary of State
Housing Action Trusts	5	Partial; focus on specific localities	From 1991 onwards; expected life of 7 years	Non-Departmental Public Body appointed by Secretary of State
Further Education Corporations	464	Cover whole of England	Corporations established 1993; previously responsibility of local education authority	Statutory corporation (exempted educational charity); first governors appointed by former governing body. Body then becomes self-appointing
Training and Enterprise Councils	75	Cover whole of England	During 1990/91 to manage contracts for Dept. of Employment	Company limited by guarantee; normally created through partnership involving Chamber of Commerce, business leaders and local authority. Appoints own board subject to conditions required by Secretary of State for Employment
Careers Service Pathfinders	13	Partial at present, but new bodies are being created as further contracts are let	Created 1993/4 to compete for and deliver contracts to provide former local authority careers services	Company limited by guarantee; normally created from partnership of local authority, TEC and Chamber of Commerce. Appoints own board
District Health Authorities	140[b]	Cover whole of England	New authorites created following 1990 Act; they are successors to authorities originally created following 1946 Act and reorganised in 1974	NHS Bodies; board includes 'non-executive' and 'executive' members; Chair appointed by Secretary of State; non-executive members appointed by Regional Health Authority
NHS Trusts	300[c]	Cover whole of England	Created in waves commencing 1991 to compete for and deliver contracts from DHAs and, subsequently, GP Fundholders; most replace the directly managed units of pre-reform district health authorities	NHS Bodies; board includes 'non-executive' members; Chair and up to 3 non-executive members appointed by Secretary of State; 2 'local community' non-executive members appointed by Regional Health Authority

Notes: a. Numbers operational at time of survey (summer 1994).
b. Numbers reducing due to amalgamations.
c. Numbers increasing as new NHS Trusts created.
Source: Skelcher and Davis, *Opening the Boardroom Door: The Membership of Local Appointed Bodies* (LGC/Joseph Rowntree Foundation, 1995).

in each type of QUANGO. In total, 1,508 questionnaires were returned giving an overall response rate of 37 per cent. This is lower than the response rate of the Widdicombe survey of local councillors[4] or the Warwick survey of DHA and NHS Trust members,[5] each of which achieved over 60 per cent. It is likely that the response rate was affected by the political climate pertaining during the research period, notably accusations of political patronage in appointments to QUANGOs, some spectacular performance failures and the creation of the Nolan Committee on Standards in Public Life. Nevertheless the large numbers of questionnaires returned, combined with the high response rate for some types of QUANGO sampled, lead us to be reasonably confident of the results. However it should be remembered that much of the data presented here is in aggregate form, and that there can be marked differences between the types of QUANGOs studied.

A number of themes are examined in this article. First we compare the structural features of local QUANGO members with those of local elected councillors, and argue that councillors' roles and the context within which they operate are much broader and more complex. Secondly the socio-economic characteristics of both groups are explored. This reveals that, when compared with councillors, local QUANGO members have a lower level of correspondence to the population as a whole. We then examine, thirdly, the recruitment and motivation of both parties, and highlight the informal appointment processes applying in local QUANGOs. Given the lack of electoral mechanisms in QUANGOs and the distance from the community, attitudes to accountability and public involvement are relevant. Our analysis of this fourth theme reveals the problematic nature of accountability for members of local QUANGOs and their self-perception of party political independence. Finally the time demands of council and local QUANGO membership are explored, illustrating the much lower time demands on QUANGO members.

COUNCILLORS AND APPOINTEES IN CONTEXT

The essential difference between local councillors and members of QUANGOs is that the former go through an electoral process while the latter are appointed to their positions (Table 2). However, there are a number of other factors consequent on this distinction. In the first place most local election campaigns are fought between candidates with party allegiances and the councils to which they are elected are nowadays normally organised on party political lines. Party politics is therefore integral to the life and role of the local councillor. This contrasts sharply with local QUANGOs which are not constituted on party political lines and where party allegiance is not, formally at least, a requirement of membership. The British electoral system operates on the basis that councillors are elected by the citizens in their ward or electoral division and as a result represent them. Consequently councillors become a focus for constituents' concerns and problems in a way that is not possible for local QUANGO members who, with a few exceptions, do not have a constituency in any clearly defined sense.

TABLE 2
COUNCILLORS AND LOCAL QUANGO MEMBERS – COMPARISON OF STRUCTURAL FEATURES

Elected Councillor	Local QUANGO Member
Must decide to stand for election	Normally invited to join board
Party political activity normally integral to role	Party political activity incidental to role
Represent constituents in particular locality	Members appointed as individuals – normally do not represent constituency
Accessible to the public	Relatively inaccessible to the public
Focus for constituents' problems with the local authority and other bodies	Not a focus for complaints or problems
Multiple service responsibilities	Single service responsibilities
Liable for surcharge	Not liable for surcharge
Formal decision-making in public	Decision-making normally in private

Councillors serve on a multi-functional body and will often, because of their role, be nominated on to other agencies – a school governing body, the management committee of a housing association, and so on. They have the opportunity to develop an awareness of the range of issues facing their locality. Local QUANGO members, however, work in a more restricted structure. The body on which they serve often deals with a single service and the possibilities for nomination on to other bodies is more limited. The councillor, therefore, is concerned with the governance of the community whilst the local QUANGO member is involved in the governance of a service. The price councillors pay is their liability for surcharge if the decisions they take are deemed to be *ultra vires*. Local QUANGO members need have no concerns here, since they are exempt from personal liability (except their limited liability where the body is constituted under the Companies Acts). The public role of the councillor is maintained when it comes to the formal arenas for debate and decision-making. Members of the public have a right of access to meetings of the council itself, as well as to its committees and sub-committees, except for matters of an individual or commercially sensitive nature. In the main QUANGOs meet in private, although there are exceptions, for example District Health Authorities (DHAs) and the statutory annual public meeting of NHS Trusts.

MEMBER CHARACTERISTICS

The caricature of the local councillor is that *he* is male, middle-aged, middle-class and white. Although broadly accurate at an aggregate level, the pattern between individual local authorities varies considerably. The same is true of the members of local QUANGOs. Overall the socio-economic characteristics of local QUANGO members are similar to those of councillors, except that they tend to be better educated formally and are less likely to live or work in the area served by their board (Table 3). However, the proportion of female members varies from 43 per cent on Housing Action Trusts (HATs) and 37 per cent on NHS Trusts to 13 per cent on Training and Enterprise Councils (TECs) and 11 per cent on Careers Service Pathfinder boards. Thirteen per cent of HAT members are black or from minority ethnic groups compared with one per cent of DHA non-executives and less than one per cent of Urban Development Corporation (UDC) members.

TABLE 3
SOCIO-ECONOMIC CHARACTERISTICS OF COUNCILLORS, LOCAL QUANGO MEMBERS AND
U.K. POPULATION

per cent	Councillors	Local QUANGO members	Population
Male	75	74	49
Female	25	26	51
Age			
18-29	6[a]	0	24
30-44	17[b]	18	27
45-59	39	55	21
60>	39	27	28
Employment			
Employed	58	73	55
Unemployed	4	1	6
Other	38	26	39
Employment sector			
Public/ voluntary	37	33	28
Private	63	67	72
Ethnic Origin			
White	n/a	97	95
Black/Asian	n/a	3	5
Location			
Live in area	n/a[c]	70	-
Work in area	n/a[c]	76	-
(Base)	(1,612)	(1,501)	-

Source: Councillor data from K. Young and N. Rao, *Coming to Terms with Change? The Local Government Councillor in 1993* (LGC/Joseph Rowntree Foundation, 1994). Local QUANGO data from Skelcher and Davis, op. cit. Data in 'population' column from 1991 Census.

Notes: *a* and *b* are figures for under 35 years and 35-44 years respectively. *c* To be eligible to stand for election, candidates must either live, work , own land or property or be a registered elector in the local authority area.

Local QUANGO members, as is the case with councillors and Members of Parliament, do not reflect the socio-economic characteristics of the population as a whole. It could be argued that seeking to construct the membership of a public body so that it broadly mirrors the community it serves is impracticable in terms of ensuring that all possible types of individuals are included, and undesirable since ability and a willingness to undertake public duty should be the prime requirements for those holding public office. However, against this should be set the view that members' characteristics tend to shape the values and experiences brought to decision making. Governmental decisions are about determining priorities which affect different groups in different ways, and it is likely that outcomes will be more responsive to the needs and requirements of the community where the board is in some way able to encompass the broad composition of its locality. Wilson and Game explore this point in relation to the under-representation of women on local councils: 'Women are the main users of council services. They make an estimated three-quarters of all calls to council departments. They are the majority of tenants, the family members who make most use of swimming pools and libraries ... They are likely to have distinctive priorities and agendas.'[6] The point is not that individuals on boards should necessarily 'represent' – that is, act to advance the interests of a group to whom they belong – but that a breadth of experience supports appropriate and responsive decision making.

There is one group that does hold a sizeable proportion of seats on local QUANGOs – members of the business community. The government has been keen to ensure that they infuse the local appointed sector, claiming that this brings to the public service their business and managerial skills. They are seen as having an important role in transforming the public service into one which operates in a more competitive environment. However, the assumption that business experience has special value in governmental decisions can be challenged. Priority setting and resource allocation in relation to the needs of the community are inherently governmental rather than managerial activities. If there is a case for special skills in the *management* of the organisation then the appropriate place to seek them is in the appointment of managers.[7]

The requirement that members of governmental bodies should have special qualifications or experience does not apply to MPs or councillors. As far back as 1960 the Herbert Commission observed that: 'The control of the expert by the amateur representing his fellow citizens is the key to the whole of our system of government.'[8] If, however, members of local QUANGOs require specialist expertise then there remains the question of what the appropriate specialisms should be. The emphasis on business skills, for example, overlooks other skills that are important in the public service. These might include the capacity to understand the needs of diverse groups and to develop policies that reflect a wider public interest.

APPOINTMENT AND ELECTION

The process by which members of local QUANGOs are appointed has normally been a 'word-of-mouth' affair, with a consequent lack of transparency about the criteria for selection. The main appointment route is the recommendation of existing board members and senior managers (Table 4). Even where the appointment is formally made by the Secretary of State, the short-list will frequently be influenced by key figures on the local QUANGO in question. The first chair of a new QUANGO commented: 'I made it clear right from the beginning that I wanted to be able to make nominations [to the Secretary of State]. I wanted to see specific experience that would help [this body].'

TABLE 4
MEMBERS' PERCEIVED SOURCE OF NOMINATION

Percentage of respondents mentioning.....	per cent
Chair, non-executives or senior managers of the body	39
Secretary of State or RHA	18
Local authority or other local public body	17
Business organisation	12
Voluntary or community organisation	7
By personal application	7
TOTAL	100
(Base)	(1,305)

Source: Skelcher and Davis, op. cit.

The significance of internal sources for the identification of new members was also identified by Ashburner and Cairncross in their study of the NHS,[9] although this is one sector that is now moving towards a more open process by advertising vacant non-executive positions and inviting individuals to apply. Members of local QUANGOs reveal a strong preference for recruitment by personal contact, 67 per cent mentioning it as one of their preferred methods. The exception to this is amongst members of urban regeneration agencies – in particular City Challenge and Housing Action Trusts – where there was a greater desire to see more formal appointment processes, including direct election. This probably reflects the fact that these two bodies, alone amongst those we studied, do have a small number of seats reserved for community or tenant directors nominated as a result of an election process. Less than a fifth of respondents preferred nomination by central government. This is important since there is a popular but incorrect impression that all QUANGO appointments are made by ministers. In fact, of the types of QUANGOs considered in our study they are only responsible for appointment to the two non-departmental public bodies and (in part) the two NHS bodies (Table 1), although they may have a veto or degree of influence in some other cases. The low level of preference for central government nomination may reflect a perception by members that they see their loyalties being to the local community – despite their lack of formal links to it – rather than to higher authority.

Underlying the recruitment process, however, is the question of members' motivation. 80 per cent of respondents mentioned public duty as a factor leading them to accept the offer of appointment, while a further 36 per cent refer to 'personal interest'. A UDC member accepted because 'I strongly support the aims this body has for my native city and I felt that this role would give me a means of putting something back into my home community' while an NHS trust non-executive thought that the work of the body 'relates to issues I'm interested in'. The picture that emerges from our study is therefore similar to the 'elite volunteers' identified in Ashburner and Cairncross's NHS study, who are 'motivated by a combination of altruism and personal development'.[10] This has some parallels with Barron *et al.*'s analysis of the motivation of local councillors.[11] They conclude that in the main candidature is less a deliberate objective and more a process of cumulative drift, where individuals who have been involved in various community activities are persuaded to stand for election. Game and Leach develop this analysis into a model of councillor recruitment. They argue that candidates for elected office have certain predispositions, including a politically active family background, acquired political skills and self-confidence. Their decision to seek election is precipitated by particular events, such as involvement in campaigns. In this process individuals develop 'a readiness to contemplate that crucial escalation of their interest, involvement and activism into a council candidature.' This readiness involves: 'Those with a sufficiently positive regard for the institutions of local government and the councillor's role, and who are or are persuaded that their current personal, family and occupational circumstances are compatible with their taking on of that role if elected.'[12]

There is a crucial difference between the two sectors, however. It is that those invited or persuaded to join a local QUANGO would (in most cases) merely be deciding to accept appointment, whereas those wishing to become a councillor must decide to subject themselves to a party selection process and then become a candidate in a local election. This latter process can be seen as a test of the individual's commitment to public service in a way that the appointment process cannot.

ACCOUNTABILITY AND PUBLIC INVOLVEMENT

Much of the debate about local QUANGOs has centred on the question of accountability. The issues are about both the nature of and mechanisms for accountability, especially in the context of the varying legal and constitutional status of appointed bodies (Table 1) and the predominance of recruitment through personal contact. Members of local QUANGOs have a clear perception of accountability *inwards* to the organisation – that is, to the chair of the board and to fellow board members (Table 5). This is likely to be because members feel accountable to those principally involved in their nomination and with whom they have a personal working relationship. However, there is also a sense of accountability *outwards* to the local community generally, and we interpret this as a consequence of the sense of public duty and service which members identified as a motivating force in accepting an appointment. Less than half of the members surveyed saw themselves as accountable to central government or to taxpayers nationally.

TABLE 5

PERCEPTIONS OF ACCOUNTABILITY BY LOCAL QUANGO MEMBERS

To whom do you consider yourself accountable? per cent respondents mentioning

Chair and non-executives	60
Local community generally	59
People who use the organisation's services	52
Secretary of State/RHA	45
Taxpayers nationally	39
Staff of the organisation	29
Chief executive	22
Nominating organisation or group	17
(Base)	(1,481)

Source: Skelcher and Davis, op. cit.

There are important differences between the eight bodies we investigated. Accountability to the community was mentioned by three in every four City Challenge directors, perhaps an indication of the specific locality focus of this type of body and the high expectations surrounding its work. This contrasts with HAT members, where three-quarters mention accountability to the chair and to the Secretary of State, in whose name their appointment is made.

Accountability is not an issue to which members of local QUANGOs give a great deal of attention. The question 'to whom do you feel accountable?' required some thought on the part of interviewees. A private sector City Challenge board director commented: '[Long pause] I've never actually been asked who I'm responsible to. [Long pause] It's an interesting one. [Pause] The community probably. [Pause] The people of [names area]. I do feel I'm trying to do something for them. Also, of course, I represent my company', while a NHS Trust non-executive reflected:

> Ah! [Pause] No, no sense of accountability. I suppose accountable to my conscience. [Long pause] I see myself as acting on behalf of patients. [Pause] Yes, if I have an accountability it's to people I've never met! And it's a feeling that [pause] that one justification for me being there is to be concerned that they get the best deal.

Others were able to answer without hesitation but still displayed differing perceptions of accountability. A Further Education (FE) college governor saw his accountability in this way: 'I was there as an individual ensuring that good governance occurred. I suppose you were doing that on behalf of the local community and the FEFC [Further Education Funding Council] – and the staff', while a HAT member commented: 'Quite simply I see myself as responsible to the Secretary of State for the use of public funds and equally responsible to the tenants who I represent – and I'm very happy with that joint responsibility!'

There is an apparent discrepancy between board members' feelings of accountability to the community and the processes by which members relate to that community. A central issue here is that 'the community' is used as a global concept rather than referring to a distinct group of individuals. What board members seem to be saying, therefore, is that they are serving the wider community through their public duties, but not any particular set of interests in the locality. This interpretation would be consistent with members' antipathy to party politics in local appointed bodies and their view that they are 'independent' members in the style of the local authorities of old (Table 6).

TABLE 6

LOCAL QUANGO MEMBERS' ATTITUDES TO THE OPERATION OF THE BOARD, BY POSITION ON THE BOARD

Please indicate your level of agreement or disagreement with the following statements...	**Mean Score**	
Range: +3=strongly agree; -3=strongly disagree	**Chairs**	**Other Members**
Non-executive directors see themselves as being independent of any political party	2.6	2.2
Greater political debate would benefit the work of this body	-2.2	-1.6

Source: Skelcher and Davis, op. cit.

TABLE 7
LOCAL QUANGO MEMBERS' ATTITUDES TO GREATER PUBLIC INVOLVEMENT IN THE
BOARD'S WORK, BY TYPE OF BODY

Greater public involvement in the board's work would be beneficial	per cent members agreeing strongly or to some extent
District Health Authority	70
Housing Action Trust	68
City Challenge	57
Training and Enterprise Council	57
Careers Pathfinder	39
NHS Trust	37
Further Education Corporation	36
Urban Development Corporation	30
(Base)	(1,462)

Source: Skelcher and Davis, op. cit.

The limited accountability mechanisms are not generally compensated by high levels of public involvement. Members overall agreed that there was little public involvement in board activities. This belief is reflected in all of the bodies except HATs, where the work of these agencies in specific localities and the role of tenant representatives on the board results in considerable levels of involvement.[13] When asked whether greater public involvement in the board's work would be beneficial, a considerable difference of opinion was revealed (Table 7). Respondents from TECs, City Challenge, DHAs and HATs felt that more public involvement would be helpful, while those from UDCs, NHS Trusts, FE Corporations and Careers Service Pathfinders were less enthusiastic. There does, therefore, seem a willingness by members on some local QUANGOs to open up the possibility of stronger links between their board and the local communities they serve.

TIME DEMANDS OF MEMBERSHIP

Membership of a local council or QUANGO makes personal demands of the individuals involved. Time is the most obvious demand. Our survey revealed that those who chair local QUANGOs spend between one and two days a week on board business with ordinary members spending half that amount. Leading councillors (that is, the Leader of the Council and majority party, and the chairs of the main committees) devote approximately twice as much time to their duties as do the chairs of local QUANGOs, while back-bench councillors spend two and a half times as much as ordinary QUANGO members (Table 8). The difference is largely accounted for by the constituency role of councillors and the greater amount of time spent in formal committee meetings, given the multi-functional nature of the local authority compared with the single-service local QUANGO. The greater time spent travelling reflects the larger geographical areas covered by many local authorities. Overall, 63 per cent of our QUANGO respondents thought that they were spending the amount of time they initially expected, while 30 per cent reported that they were devoting more time.

TABLE 8
TIME COMMITMENT OF LOCAL QUANGO MEMBERS AND COUNCILLORS

Hours	All activities	Formal meetings	Contact with public	Meetings with managers	Preparation and travel	Other
Local QUANGO chairs	46	9	4	11	12	10
Leading councillors	86	25	17	8	21	15
Ordinary QUANGO members	26	7	3	4	6	6
Backbench councillors	65	19	15	4	16	11

Source: Councillor data from Young and Rao, op. cit., table 3.3. 'Contact with public' is a composite of 'electors' problems' and 'public consultation' columns in Young and Rao's table. Local QUANGO member data from Skelcher and Davis, op. cit.

There are limitations on the extent to which local QUANGO members are able or willing to devote more time to their board duties. One commented that his ability to contribute effectively to board discussions and decisions was limited by his time availability:

> You tend to roll up once a month to board meetings. I always read the papers and try to work out ahead of time what's happening. I will occasionally ring an officer. But I have not been willing to make the step and devote a lot of time and energy ... If I wanted to say to the chair 'Look, I want a bigger role' he wouldn't say no. But I'm not willing to spend 8 or 10 hours a week to get into the organisation and learn all the issues.

He went on to comment that the local councillors who were board members were amongst the most involved, since 'they are full-time and we are part-time'. It is likely that the local contacts and briefing available to council members from their own authorities also supports their effective involvement on a board.

CONCLUSION

Our analysis has illustrated the more substantial role of local councillors, and in particular their greater level of public contact and their wider range of service responsibilities. Whether an individual is appointed or elected has relatively little effect on member characteristics at an aggregate level, despite the possibility for the former to produce a composition that is more reflective of the community at large. However, local councillors go through a more complex recruitment process and have a greater level of local accountability because of the formal electoral system and informal party and constituency links. The discussion produces a conundrum: why do some individuals take the path to become local councillors while others wait for the invitation to join a local QUANGO? Our survey revealed that one in five local QUANGO members had stood for election as a councillor, although only one in ten currently held such a position. There is, therefore, a degree of overlap between the group of individuals willing to enter local politics and those who agree to public service in an appointed capacity. When we asked local QUANGO members what discouraged them from standing for election as a councillor the main reasons were a dislike of local government politics (49 per cent) and lack of time (44 per cent). The membership of a local QUANGO is perceived as both less political and less onerous than that of a local authority.

However, even though many respondents have said that they are independent of party politics it should not be concluded that they are politically independent. Patronage through the appointments system, as well as the desire by the government to see greater private sector involvement, all contribute to the possibility of one set of political interests predominating amongst board members. Peck's analysis of TECs, for example, illustrates how business involvement is seen as depoliticising the local governance of training.[14] This depoliticisation occurs under the guise of 'independent' members who bring their individual experience and good judgement to public services outside the local democratic arena. This analysis has a ring of familiarity to local government ears, since it is the view promoted by independent councillors, who used to be many but are now few in number. Local QUANGO members' perception of party political independence, therefore, should be set within a wider political analysis which would lead to questions about the extent to which particular interests are excluded or marginalised in board recruitment, in the process of board decision-making and in the outcomes of decisions. The articulation of 'independence' can conceal a real set of political interests whose existence is clouded by the lack of openness and local accountability of the membership of these local appointed bodies.

NOTES

1. See, for instance, S. Weir and W. Hall (eds.), *EGO Trip: Extra-Governmental Organisations in the United Kingdom and their Accountability* (Charter 88 Trust, 1994); H. Davis and J. Stewart, *The Growth of Government by Appointment: Implications for Local Democracy* (Local Government Management Board, 1993).
2. R. Morris, *Central and Local Control After the Education Reform Act 1988* (Longman, 1990).
3. C. Skelcher and H. Davis, *Opening the Boardroom Door: The Membership of Local Appointed Bodies* (LGC/Joseph Rowntree Foundation, 1995).
4. Widdicombe Report, *The Conduct of Local Authority Business*, Cmnd 9799 (HMSO, 1986).
5. L. Ashburner and L. Cairncross, 'Membership of the New Style Health Authorities: Continuity or Change', *Public Administration* 71 (Autumn 1993).
6. D. Wilson and C. Game, *Local Government in the United Kingdom* (Macmillan, 1994), p.212.
7. J. Stewart and H. Davis, 'A New Agenda for Local Governance', *Public Money and Management*, 14(4) (1994).
8. Herbert Commission, *The Royal Commission on Local Government in Greater London*, Cmnd 1164 (1960), para. 233.
9. Ashburner and Cairncross, op. cit.
10. Ibid.
11. J. Barron, G. Crawley and T. Wood, 'Drift and Resistance: Refining Models of Political Recruitment', *Policy and Politics* 17(3) (1989).
12. C. Game and S. Leach, *Councillor Recruitment and Turnover: An Approaching Precipice?* (Local Government Management Board, 1993), p.16.
13. J. Chumrow, 'HATs: A Possible Role Model?', *Parliamentary Affairs* 48(2) (1995).
14. J. Peck, 'The Trouble with TECs', *Policy and Politics* 21(4) (1993).

Business as Usual? The New Police Authorities and the Police and Magistrates' Courts Act

BARRY LOVEDAY

In 1993, the Home Secretary, Kenneth Clarke was to publish a White Paper on Police Reform designed to radically alter the structure of police authorities and the government of the police service in England and Wales. This was based on an official perception that contemporary demands placed on the police required more powerful and businesslike police authorities, to give leadership to the police and ensure that money was spent more effectively. In his statement on the police to the House of Commons the Home Secretary outlined a set of proposals, which, had they been implemented, would have dramatically changed the central local relationship of the government of the police.[1]

In his original proposals, Kenneth Clarke was effectively to recommend the implementation of a central government patronage system for the police service. Had this been introduced, it would have overtly politicised both local police authorities and their police forces. In recommending the reform of police authorities, he planned to reduce police authority membership to an initial 16 members, of which half would be selected by the Home Secretary, including the chairman of each local police authority (LPA). Such selection was to have been made unilaterally by the Home Office, and also made to a diminishing number of police authorities as massive police force amalgamations, originally planned to cut the number from 43 to around 22 forces, enabled the government to abolish what were expected to be necessarily many redundant police authorities.[2]

As an example of the centralising nature of the Thatcher and Major governments, the original plans for the police service demonstrated a continuing commitment to the elimination of local responsibility for local services. Within the local government world it was fully expected that the retention of eight councillors on each authority was intended to be a temporary phenomenon, as the legislation paid insufficient attention to how a democratic balance of the councillor membership could be accomplished in local policing areas.[3]

Barry Loveday, University of Portsmouth

Never a minister to be overly concerned with constitutional niceties, Kenneth Clarke clearly planned to create police authorities which were, in terms of their responsibilities, not unlike the Hospital Trust, which the same minister established when at the Department of Health. The proposal for the police appeared to Conservative back-benchers to be quite unremarkable. They were apparently ready to accept the potential politicisation of the police service on the basis of ministerial claims that this would improve the efficiency of another 'failing public service'. It is, of course, a matter of record that the Major government at no time shared the adulation towards the police demonstrated by Mrs Thatcher during her period of office. While senior ministers in the Major government supported the police in public, in private they were to be bitterly resentful of the perceived failure of the police. As a former Home Secretary was to comment, they felt that the police had failed the government on the crime problem despite increased expenditure heaped on the police service during the 1980s.[4]

The White Paper on Police Reform demonstrated the government's solution to both the crime problem and the apparent failure of the police. This was to be the introduction of social market principles into the police service to encourage it to fight crime more efficiently.[5] In what was to prove to be a traumatic experience for the police service, one which had come to assume automatic support from Conservative governments, the combined impact of the Sheehy Inquiry and White Paper on Police Reform ended what had become a mutually supportive relationship between the police and the Conservatives.[6] In a report which was clearly designed to de-stabilise established police interests, the Sheehy Inquiry into Police Responsibilities and Rewards was to recommend fixed contracts for all police officers, structural severance, performance pay and local wage bargaining. These constituted just four of over 200 recommendations made in its report to the Home Secretary. The new managerialism which was propounded in the White Paper on police reform was also closely linked to the Sheehy recommendations for radical internal reform of police management.

Fortunately for the police service, a mixture of luck, government misjudgement and the departure of Kenneth Clarke from the Home Office was to mean that the full weight of reform proposed by that minister was not to be experienced by them. As Home Secretary, Michael Howard has proved to be more cautious in his dealings with the police service, particularly in relation to implementing the Sheehy proposals. Moreover the government's misjudgement in pushing its police legislation to the House of Lords, rather than the Commons, provided an opportunity for amending the most potentially damaging clauses in the original Police and Magistrates' Courts' Bill.

NOMINATION POWERS

In the House of Lords, immediate cross-bench resistance to legislation which, if passed, would have centralised control of the police service, became apparent early on. In a series of amendments designed to dilute the more extreme centralising clauses, indirect nomination of independent members was to be forced upon the government. Additionally, police authority members would themselves select the chairperson. A Home Office alternative involving the County Lords Lieutenant in selection of independents, while demonstrating a desperate commitment by government to evade electoral accountability, proved to be entirely unacceptable to both the House of Lords and Lords Lieutenant. Further dilution of overt central control was to be achieved by giving elected members a simple majority on the new police authorities. It was accepted that the LPAs would have nine elected members, five independent and three magistrate members. In a limited number of LPAs, the total number of members was increased to 19. This was necessary if entire local districts were not to be left unrepresented by an elected councillor.

The government was also forced to abandon direct ministerial nomination. Instead, an arcane, complex and elongated procedure was to be introduced to identify independent members. In a time-consuming process, a nomination panel made up of a Home Office nominee, a police authority nominee and one other chosen by the first two, was made responsible for identifying a 'short list' of 20 possible independent nominees. The selection process followed on from a exercise in which places on the LPA were to be advertised in the local press and/or where specific individuals were invited to apply. The agreed short-list would be forwarded to the Home Secretary, who would then short-list ten of the original 20 nominees. The 'shortened short-list' would be returned to the local nomination team, who were made immediately responsible for selecting five independent members from the Home Secretary's short-list.

The justification for the introduction of independent nominees was to be outlined in some detail in 1993 by the Home Secretary, Michael Howard. At the ACPO Local Authority Association, Birmingham Conference that year, he was to argue that nomination provided the best opportunity for a more representative cross-section of the community to serve on LPAs. Those not fully represented in the past included, he claimed 'shopkeepers, teachers and farmers' who would join businessmen as potential nominees to reformed LPAs. Yet as a Local Authority Association survey was to demonstrate, prior to the introduction of the Police and Magistrates Courts Act 1994 (PMCA), businessmen were in fact well represented already on existing police authorities.[7] Additionally, most LPAs could, depending on geographic location, identify shopkeepers, teachers and farmers, who served on the unreformed police authorities. The rather spurious claims made by the Home Secretary, were, however, to serve as the government's justification for the wholesale reduction of democratically locally elected members on police authorities. This selection procedure was, it was suspected, originally to have been the forerunner of plans to remove the elected element entirely from LPAs.[8]

SELECTION OF INDEPENDENT MEMBERS

Detailed analysis of the selection of independent members cannot be attempted here. It is sufficient to note that experiences of the selection procedure differed markedly between LPAs. Some problems experienced by LPAs were self-generated while others were to be explained by overt central government interference. In Cleveland, an extremely low profile publicity campaign to advertise independent places on the LPA was to result in the government determining the short-list of independents. In what proved to be a cataclysmic misjudgement, the decision of the county council to provide a minimum number of nominees was ultimately to lead to the removal of the Labour chairman from the LPA and his replacement by a Conservative. Elsewhere, the selection process was to be challenged in the House of Lords. In Warwickshire, it was claimed, government whips and business managers had been consulted in the selection of nominees.[9] A 'balanced list' of nominees, identified jointly by the county council and chief constable, was to be rejected by the Home Office. The overt, partisan nature of the government's intervention in Warwickshire was to lead to a complaint from the chief constable to the Home Secretary, although this appeared to have no affect at all on the Home Secretary's final decision.[10] Indeed, the selection process for Warwickshire was to provide a guide to the general principles which informed government vetting of the police authority short-lists. In Warwickshire, nominees from Labour strongholds, members of the ethnic community and women were to be deleted from the nomination list sent to the Home Secretary. Those who reached the final short-list were overwhelmingly professional self-employed or businessmen. In a survey conducted by the University of Portsmouth, which sought to identify the backgrounds of independent members, the overall strategy of the government became clearer.[11] Thus in the shire counties the immediate characteristics of those reaching the final selection stage was that they were overwhelmingly white, middle-aged, middle-class males. Additionally, the majority of those selected were not farmers, teachers or shopkeepers but either self-employed professionals, business executives or recently retired managers from private companies. A significant number of retired senior military officers also joined the new LPAs as independent members. [12]

THE INDEPENDENT MEMBERS

The University of Portsmouth survey identified a cross-section of reformed LPAs and the backgrounds and interests of their independent members. In Humberside, four of the independent members are drawn from business backgrounds, the fifth is a teacher. In Staffordshire, independent members include a tax accountant, a retired chief executive of a building society and two self-employed business consultants. In Gloucestershire, the independent members consist of an Asian businessman, a retired brigadier, a retired manager from the electricity industry, a retired police officer and a manager from a Health Authority. Lincolnshire demonstrates an interesting feature among independents, which is the large number who have retired from business or are of pensionable age. In that county, for example, the independent members consist of a retired accountant, a retired assistant dock master, a retired managing director; and a retired army officer. The one non-pensionable member is a private-sector manager.

The armed services are also well represented on the new LPAs. Kent, Lincolnshire and Warwickshire now boast retired brigadiers, whilst in Wiltshire, other than a chartered accountant, the independent members consist of two retired military officers, a senior army administrator and a senior civil servant from the Ministry of Defence. Yet the overwhelming characteristic is the incidence of either self-employed or recently retired businessmen. In Thames Valley, independent members include an accountant, a management consultant, a financial consultant, a former manager from Marks & Spencer and a former manager with Grand Met plc (now self-employed). In Warwickshire, the independents consist, *inter alia*, of an international businessman who is a consultant to government departments, a brigadier (who is a chair of an NHS trust), a retired industrial relations manager and a lecturer from University of Warwick Business School. In Cheshire, the independents include a retired personnel director from ICI, a solicitor and a chief executive of the Chamber of Commerce. While, therefore, the selection of independents may not have entirely met the criteria set out by Michael Howard in his Birmingham speech, it does appear to have amply achieved those of his predecessor who wanted to recruit businessmen to the new police authorities. Any expectation (if it existed) that this process would bring a broad cross-section of the community onto police authorities has not been realised. The process has reinforced an existing bias towards white, male, middle-aged and middle-class members of the community serving on LPAs. In Northamptonshire, a similar bias has been identified by the current chairperson, Dr Marie Dickie. While two ethnic community members, originally selected by the LPA, did survive the Home Office 'weeding' process, only one of the women on the initial list did so. Moreover, any attempt to provide a geographical balance within the county was to be completely unsuccessful and the one candidate from the most industrial and deprived area of the county was ruled out by the Home Office.[13] Elsewhere, active trade unionists were to be eliminated by the Home Office in drawing up the 'shortened short-list' of independent nominees.

THE SELECTION PROCESS OF INDEPENDENT MEMBERS

Inevitably, the very number and different experiences of LPAs makes generalisation concerning the selection process difficult. It would appear however, that for many LPA clerks, the process of advertising and targeting of individuals and companies inevitably dictated the likely make-up of independents on the new LPAs. Many LPA panels were to target voluntary organisations, prominent individuals in the community and business organisations as they were encouraged to do by Home Office guidance.[14]

The process was effectively left by the Home Office to LPA clerks to co-ordinate. It was later to be described by one of them as 'chaotic' and a process which was 'cobbled together in the absence of clear guidance from the centre'. Yet the panels were constrained by identification of 'qualities sought' among independent members by Home Office guidance. As well as being of 'good character', the independent members were expected to possess 'good communication and financial skills'; to be able to demonstrate the ability to challenge accepted views in a constructive way', and to understand the pressures and challenges confronting the police themselves. They were also expected to demonstrate 'skills and experience' which would 'broaden the expertise' available to the authority.[15] This criterion could be safely guaranteed to exclude the low waged, unskilled and working class members of the community, those indeed, most likely to have some experience of being policed within the community. Instead, this process of selection placed a premium on those with a private sector background and membership of the professional middle-class. This is clearly reflected in the current makeup of independents on LPAs.

CONFLICTING VIEWS OF THE NEW LPA

One of the more interesting features of the new LPA arrangements is the differing views expressed by those able to compare old and new police authorities. Limited evidence to date suggests that the new LPAs have won the approval of many senior local government officers who have a continued responsibility for police authority business. One view expressed is that the reformed LPAs could enhance the role of the police authority and

provide greater direction and purpose to the work of the LPA. Little
evidence exists to suggest that either the nomination system or the
introduction of independents has been universally condemned or rejected.
One local government officer was to conclude that the new police
authorities, released from county council control, provided a 'breath of fresh
air' by enabling a smaller number of members to become 'very focused' on
policing issues. For one clerk, the new police authorities were seen as being
'more focused, better sized, more businesslike and better able to address the
issues quickly'. The reduced size of the authority, while creating problems
of representation, appeared to have created a more executive decision
making forum. A chief constable was to suggest that it was much easier to
work with 17 than 35 members which had been the norm prior to the Police
and Magistrates' Courts Act (PMCA).[16] A smaller number of members had
helped create, it was thought, a better working relationship than was
experienced with the former LPAs. These were to be viewed as cumbrous
bodies, many of whose members often had only a peripheral interest in
policing. Moreover, despite the experience of direct intervention in some
LPA selection processes by Home Office, it was felt that the process of
selection was not one that could be closely managed by that Department.
Perhaps 'more by default than conspiracy or design' it was felt that the new
LPA structures appeared to be potentially more effective than those they
replaced.[17] Within one police authority association, attention has been drawn
to a number of people already prominent in public life, who have been
appointed as independent members of police authorities. They can
confidently be expected to make an effective contribution to the police
authority's work, which can only serve the wider public good. Elsewhere,
chief officers and chairpersons have identified a more searching and
enquiring interest in policing issues among new LPA members than
characterised former LPA members. In many LPAs seminar sessions on
policing have been held both jointly with the chief officer and
independently by the LPA. Elsewhere, one chief constable was to note that
police authority meetings lasted, on average, over four hours and had
provided ample opportunity for all members to contribute to LPA business,
often in a very detailed fashion. In Cheshire, the clerk to the police authority
was to describe the new arrangements as 'eminently workable'. He believed
that the new LPAs may provide an effective model for the future.
Increasingly the LPA was seen as not being a 'party political animal'. In
Cheshire, the occasions where votes were taken and counted had proved to
be minimal. Usually, a consensus view was sought in place of the partisan
division which had characterised, former LPA business.[18] Moreover, given
the size of the Cheshire police authority, it acted in plenary whenever it
could by not establishing an over-elaborate committee structure. In

Cheshire, the full police authority meets on seven occasions a year, although this includes two performance review committee meetings of the full LPA. Two committees, a general purposes and complaints and personnel committee now constitute the total committee structure.

ELECTED AND INDEPENDENT MEMBERS

A frequent comment made by officers concerning relations between elected and independent members identified the very 'positive relationship' which had developed between the two. As the clerk to the Cheshire LPA has argued in relation to independents: 'My own experience in Cheshire is that (independent members) bring specialist experience and skills which effectively complement the wider experience in public life of the elected members and magistrates.'[19]

This was balanced by specific cases where serious problems had arisen between councillors and independent members. In Warwickshire the work of the LPA was threatened early on by the unilateral demand made by one independent member that the LPA should be removed entirely from local government and that elected members should not chair the LPA. In Thames Valley, independent members were to argue strongly for the creation of an association of LPAs independent of local government which would differentiate them from their predecessor bodies. The recognition that police authorities were separate from local government led to a recognition, within the Association of County Councils, that new machinery was needed at national level to represent them. This led to an independent committee, the Committee of Local Police Authorities (CoLPA) being established. CoLPA is still addressing its traditional links with local government and the needs of a national representative body for all police authorities. The future relationship with the Local Government Association will be a challenging issue in the coming months. The long-term significance of independent members on LPAs has yet to be realised but this can be expected to change if they begin to take over the chairs of LPAs. This is quite likely where LPA councillors reflect local partisan strength and where there can be no necessary expectation that elected members will vote *en bloc* for one of their number as chairperson. One chief constable has expressed concern over the potential influence of 'maverick elected members' who, for partisan reasons, vote for independents or magistrates to chair the LPA.[20] Evidence that this has already occurred is provided by the replacement of Labour chairs by magistrate members or, in some cases, by Conservative members. Overall, the PMCA appears to have been introduced at the expense of local Labour control of a number of LPAs. Gains by magistrates or Conservatives have been very largely at Labour's expense. Moreover, the

narrow majority enjoyed by elected members over appointed members
effectively guarantees future instability or the selection of independents to
chairs. This must be the logical consequence of a system which requires
absolute proportionality in terms of elected party representation but yet
places a premium on the selection of businessmen. This might be expected
to discriminate in favour of those who hold political views and allegiances
at one particular end of the political spectrum.

Relations between elected and independent members in a number of
LPAs remains uncertain. The new LPAs have effectively destroyed the
natural political majorities which formerly sustained elected chairs. There is
now a need for chairs to court all members of the LPA. In this situation it
becomes important to keep the independent members 'on side'. In Cheshire,
a Liberal Democrat and a Labour member were to be asked by the
independents about their aims as potential chairmen of the LPA. In
Northamptonshire there has been a conscious commitment by the Labour
chair to encourage and support the independent LPA members. As has
become very quickly clear to those involved, the LPAs are now not like any
traditional local government committee. They have to be handled very
differently. As one LPA clerk was to suggest, 'the old order' had been
challenged by the arrival of the independents and this had to be respected
by elected chairs.[21] One aim of government policy was to secure political
balance amongst the councillor members of the police authority, while
removing politics from the police authority agenda. Under the new
structure, the practice of group meetings prior to authority meetings is
thought to have ceased in some areas. With their new planning
responsibilities, police authorities are developing new relationships with
local forces and becoming more inquisitorial bodies.

Councillor membership and the composition of the elected element on
the LPAs does continue to present problems. The requirement for political
balance has had some interesting consequences for Conservative
representation on the LPA. Because the PMCA was silent on the distribution
of places, their present composition reflects the fact that urban areas are
better represented than rural areas. As a result, the representation of Labour
and Liberal Democrats can always be expected to be greater (among elected
members) than Conservative members. In Thames Valley, Sussex,
Wiltshire, Avon and Somerset and North Yorkshire, the impact of this bias
towards urban representation has meant that the ability of the LPA to
achieve political balance has proved difficult. In the metropolitan areas,
where there are greater natural majorities, this issue is of less significance,
although in the West Midlands the Conservatives have no elected
representative from Birmingham, the biggest and most highly populated
authority in the area. Within the counties, any further reorganisation of local

government will be likely to reinforce their political imbalance. Elsewhere the severely limited elected representation provided by the PMCA has clearly been demonstrated. In the biggest conurbations, whole metropolitan districts are now represented by just one elected member. In the shires, some districts with populations of over 100,000 originally failed to achieve elected representation on the LPA. If, therefore, small and more businesslike LPAs have been established, this has been achieved at the cost of some legitimacy and authority which is conferred by election. In terms of police authority representation, it has also effectively disenfranchised many communities.

LOCAL POLICE AUTHORITY RESPONSIBILITIES

The PMCA gives the police authority significant and new responsibilities. It will be responsible, in conjunction with the chief constable, for developing an annual Local Policing Plan (LPP), which will identify both national and local policing objectives. It will also require the chief constable to cost his activities and will, on the basis of Home Office Circular 27/94, mean that ultimate responsibility for the LPP will rest with the police authority. Thus it is stated in that circular: 'Responsibility for the final content of the plan will rest with the police authority' (para.4).

To forward the LPP and ensure that local objectives are set, a primary duty is given to the LPA to ensure that adequate local consultation is made with local communities. The consultation mechanism is provided by the Police Consultative Groups established under Section 106 of the Police and Criminal Evidence Act (1984). Additionally, the LPA may be required to set targets for police forces to meet in terms of local (or national) objectives. They will also be required to produce an annual report which will identify the extent to which the police and police authority fulfilled their statutory duties and achieved objectives set out in the LPP. LPAs will also have responsibility for introducing contract arrangements for chief officers and the application of performance-related pay. These 'businesslike' responsibilities are, in effect, the justification for the reduction in membership of LPAs. Yet in one simple but significant way the new LPAs do not appear to have real power or ultimate responsibility for what the police do. Under the PMCA, the power of the purse appears to have been effectively denied to the LPA. The PMCA gives the chief constable ultimate responsibility for finance and does not establish the purchaser/provider split which the Major government has found to be so necessary in all other public services. Indeed, the failure to introduce this element of social market principles into the relationship between police and LPA could prove to be a major weakness for police authorities. Within the PMCA there is no requirement to employ support staff for the LPA other than that of a clerk and treasurer. If the LPA decides that in order to fulfil its role it needs to employ a secretariat and advisers, the prior agreement of the chief constable may be needed.

Government policy, enshrined in the Police and Magistrates' Courts Act, is that the dedicated staffing of a police authority needs the agreement of the chief constable and, in the absence of such agreement, determination by the Secretary of State. At the time when the legislation was passing through parliament, the local authority associations sought to challenge the position on the basis that this would undermine the ability of the police authority to act independently. It remains to be seen whether in practice these fears were well founded. Within the 1964 Police Act no such powers were given to the chief constable and the LPA could employ any advisers it might wish (a power only rarely used, it must be said). While, therefore, individual consultants might be contracted by the LPA to advise it on the development of LPPs, this would be for a strictly limited period.[22]

The issue of LPA employment of advisers could be a central issue to the long-term effectiveness of the LPA. If the LPA is to act independently, it will need to have more than information provided by the police force when developing local policing plans. Moreover, the long-term need for independent advisers has been recognised by some clerks. The clerk of one authority was, for example, to comment on the need for 'an independent check to assess the chief constable's plan and also help the LPA assess police performance'. Central to the role of the LPA was the issue of 'audit', which involved the LPA in much more than just the mechanistic approach of performance indicators. This, one clerk argued, would require dedicated research staff and it was his opinion that the issue of an independent secretariat was likely to arise in many LPAs in the future.[23] Yet the constraint could prove to be that the LPA would not want to divert police finance to its own activities. At the present time most LPAs have adopted a minimalist approach and have accepted low on-going costs in terms of administrative support. Problems could arise, however, in relation to independent advice, consultative arrangements and the preparation of the first annual reports by the LPA. Any refusal to invest in LPA support services could also raise doubts about the ability of the LPA to fulfil its statutory responsibilities.

ANNUAL REPORTS AND LOCAL POLICING PLANS

As with the initial selection process of independents, no guidance had been provided by the Home Office on the preparation of the police authority annual report. In at least one county the expectation is that the chief constable's and police authority annual report will be published in one document. The annual report will ultimately follow on from an evaluation of police performance based on the local plan. In 1994/95, most LPPs were effectively drawn up by the chief constable for the year with only minor input being provided by most LPA members. This can be expected to change quite substantially in relation to plans for the year 1996/97 where LPAs will expect to be fully involved. As the clerk to the Cheshire Police Authority has argued:

> Authorities played a relatively passive role in the planning process. They had to rely on the work led by the chief constables which had identified core policing priorities to fit in with the national and local objectives. The local plan process requires must more of the authority this year. This means members need a greater in-depth knowledge of local policing issues. This includes organisational staffing, and equipment issues as well as understanding patterns of crime in the area.[24]

It will be a matter of interest to discover how much independent advice and administrative support will be directed to the LPA. Yet the Local Policing Plan could be best viewed as the crucial fulcrum of police force accountability. In drawing up the preliminary draft, the chief constable will be required identify national objectives and any targets set by government which they are encouraged to meet. The plan must reflect local objectives and these will be ascertained by a process of local consultation. Although the PMCA does not confine consultation with the community to police consultative groups, it is clear that as presently constituted these bodies may not always provide a representative reflection of community views to the police authority. They, rather like the new LPAs, are often white, male, middle class and middle aged in membership and can be dependent on the local police force for their continued survival.[25] As Erica Stratta has argued elsewhere, in relation to PCGs they specifically do not include those people who are most often likely to be in contact with operational policing. That is not to say that in some cases consultative groups do not work well and may inject views of their own in to the policy process. It is, however, of some concern that, while a growing consensus among practitioners appears to be that alternative mechanisms of consultation need to be found, HMIC are in fact increasingly demanding that all police forces should establish police consultative groups when more useful alternatives have already been discovered.[26]

COMMUNITY CONSULTATION

Community consultation presents a further problem for LPAs. As one chief constable of a county force was to comment, while it was easier to work with 17 rather than 35 members on an LPA, there was very much greater pressure on members to sustain an effective consultation programme. The reduced size of LPAs meant there could be more work than members could reasonably be expected to take on. One unforeseen consequence of targeting businessmen onto LPAs as independents had also become apparent. Businessmen, it has been discovered, are themselves often very busy and find it difficult to sustain community consultative and other responsibilities. As a chief constable noted, four of his five independent members worked and of these three 'had high-powered jobs'.[27] It is something of an irony to discover that it is businessmen who, encouraged to join the LPA, may find it difficult to fulfil their responsibilities under the PMCA. This suggests that consultative arrangements, a central plank in the government's defence of police authority reform and demanding in time, will need to be reviewed. While the Home Office has initiated research on community consultation, LPAs may need to consider alternatives to Section 106 PACE committees.

One attractive structure has been identified in Northamptonshire. Here the LPA chairperson has recently argued that effective consultation can be developed by the creation of district community safety committees, hosted by district or borough councils, in agreement with the police authority. In the model for consultation developed in Northamptonshire, a community safety forum (or committee) provides a solution to two weaknesses of the existing police consultative groups. As the chair of Northamptonshire has argued, these weaknesses reflected the fact that: 'They were toothless and they were invisible. Now the demands of local people for better street lighting, for security doors on council flats, more visible police patrols, can have a real focus and some practical end results can be seen.'[28]

More significantly, the use of district and borough committees might provide a degree of legitimacy, authority and access denied to wholly nominated bodies. Whether all LPAs adopt the Northampton model remains a matter of interest. A central defence of reform was to provide effective consultation with the community. If this is an objective then something along the lines of the Northamptonshire model would need to be considered. This becomes more important as the link between police authority and local government itself becomes more tenuous. All LPAs are now independent corporate bodies with their own budget and standard spending assessment. They are under no requirement to make use of former local government staff and can appoint from elsewhere should they wish to do so.

CHIEF OFFICER RELATIONS

The reaction to the PMCA among chief officers is probably best described as mixed. If the PMCA has given a new financial freedom to chief officers, this has been more than balanced by a range of measures which they believe threaten to centralise the police service significantly. The centralising pressures do not just emanate from national objectives set annually by the Home Secretary, although they do represent the most overt statutory intervention to date into constabulary independence. Changes in funding of police forces, which have ended the automatic provision by the Home Office of 51 per cent of spending on the police force, may also prove to be significant. A new grant mechanism which identifies a fixed cash limited standard spending assessment (SSA) for each police force has ended any safety net which might cover possible overspends in a financial year. County council support by virement to (rather than from) police forces, has ended. In at least one police force county support for the police pension fund had been significant in the past. One chief officer has also argued that the requirement to provide the Home Secretary and LPA with 'costed plans', threatens to introduce a central financial straightjacket at precisely the time when flexibility was being encouraged by way of devolved budgets. He believed that costed plans were a means of exercising greater central control over policing; that they were largely treasury-driven and designed to push down police expenditure. When costed plans were linked to increased intervention by a Home Secretary, in what were essentially tactical rather than strategic policing issues, there was, he believed, a real threat to locally accountable policing. 'Interference by edict' and the setting of targets for national objectives was tantamount to encouraging the Home Secretary to interfere openly in operational policing matters.[29]

The identification of 'targets' had other consequences which were equally worrying to chief officers. Setting of national objectives and targets could 'skew police performance' and also give a spurious credibility to activities which ultimately only served to mislead the public. As one chief officer noted, the limited value of performance measures was demonstrated in relation to the national objective relating to detection of 'violent crime'. The most successful police force would be one operating in an area where recorded violent crime was already high and which was able to meet such targets. While 'targeting' known criminals had impacted on crime rates, the novelty value of police proactive targeting, in his opinion, would be of only limited duration as criminals 'began to figure out how the police were achieving the detections'. Among chief officers there also appeared to be little support or credibility given to government claims that bar charts and performance leagues would improve either the efficiency or accountability of the police service. There was also a concern that the Home Office orientation towards measurement of performance could ultimately undermine the crucial relationship between police and community. The central feature of government policy appeared to be its political encouragement to interfere in local policing. Home Office officials were aware of the dangers of such an approach but 'they were too scared to tell the Home Secretary of their concerns'. It appeared to some that now only chief police officers 'were prepared to tell the Home Secretary the truth'. For a number of chief officers, therefore, the single most important test for the new LPAs would be whether they too became committed to national objectives and league tables or whether they 'would be brave enough to say that their force did not have to be top of the league'.[30] Certainly the consensus among clerks and chairs is to doubt the value of measuring police activity. As with other public services, it is difficult to ascertain clear links between inputs and outputs when so many extraneous factors may influence events over which the police service has no control. There is, in addition, a growing interest within ACPO to directing attention to 'outcomes' rather than 'outputs' as a more useful indicator of overall police performance.[31]

There is no clear consensus among chief officers as to the benefits to police of the PMCA. New freedoms given by the Act are balanced by the real threat of more overt central interference in local policing. Central intervention can now even extend to police authorities, as has been recently discovered in Staffordshire. Here, LPA planning will be open to inspection by HMIC. It is argued by HMIC that he may inspect LPAs' planning and judge their efficiency. As an agent of the Home Secretary, HMIC will be naturally interested in the degree to which LPAs conform to a model encouraged by the centre. The apparent ability of HMIC to inspect the LPA raises quite fundamental questions concerning the accountability and future of the police authority as an independent body.[32]

CONCLUSION

What picture of the new role of LPAs is provided to date by this 'snapshot' of their work? The introduction of independent members has not met with universal opposition by those experienced in LPA business. One official suggested, that 'by political compromise they had produced a system which may well influence the future shape of policing'. This novel process of accountability could actually contribute to improving the public accountability of the police service. The search for consensus in which members, elected and nominated, worked together was also a new feature within the LPA. This reflected a noticeable pressure towards fusion between chief officers and the police authority. Government interest in such fusion has been manifested most recently by Home Office minister, David McLean. In extolling the virtues of the new LPAs he has argued that:

> The new authorities are leaner, meaner and more interested in policing than politics. They will have an impact. It has already started and they

are a formidable force for action against crime. The new authorities include independent people. They will add invaluable experience to complement the magistrates and councillors who will make up an awesome team .[33]

The optimism exhibited by the minister is not however altogether shared by chief officers, who might have been expected to benefit most from the PMCA. While a number of local government officers had concluded that the new system had worked well and that the new LPAs could be more businesslike and effective, this opinion was not shared by chief officers. For them it was apparent that the success of the nomination process had been entirely dependent on what could be a passing phenomenon. Its success was explained by those selectors of the initial list of nominees being drawn from opposition political parties of a very different colour to that controlling the government. The fact that Labour and Liberal Democrat members had drawn up the original nomination list meant that the Home Secretary could exercise only a limited discretion by identifying a shortened 'short list'. But, as one chief officer argued, what situation would arise if those selecting independent nominees locally were members of the same party which controlled central government? In 1994, members of local opposition party selected initial nominations and identified the final nominees and any 'balance' achieved was probably a result of this. Yet in future, a similar situation could not always be expected to obtain. As a result, the institutional structure was 'highly dangerous', as it might give the opportunity to a central governing party to emasculate a balanced membership if the same party was in office locally. Nor did the chief officers see the 'downsizing' of LPAs as always a benefit in terms of decision making. Some saw less representation as a democratic loss. Moreover, if the system appeared to work, this depended more on individuals than structures. There were also 'huge uncertainties' about the nomination process. Neither LPAs nor chief officers would know who would put up for nomination next time round, or if 50 per cent of the nominees selected were 'dumped off by that minister' what criteria would be used by the Home Secretary. They would not know who the Home Secretary would be who made that decision or the political persuasion of those choosing nominees. The whole procedure was in the view of one chief officer a 'hostage to fortune'.

Some chief officers were to express regret about the withdrawal of LPAs from local government. For one chief officer there was a conscious commitment on his part to involve the county council closely in the development of local policing plans. A view was also expressed that, while the financial break with the county council now meant there was greater certainty in terms of police finance, now there was 'nowhere else to turn if the money ran out'.[34] Nor was there any apparent consensus among chief officers on the perceived benefits of performance related pay. In one force, ACPO rank officers have jointly agreed that PRP was collectively unacceptable. If awarded PRP, 'they would hand it back to the police authority'. PRP was seen as potentially damaging to the police service and one chief officer expressed the view that his force would actively seek to avoid paying any performance awards to individual officers because of the potential divisiveness this might engender.

The issue of PRP and contracts when added to performance league tables could prove to be early tests of the kind of fusion between chief officers and LPAs which the government wishes to achieve. Given the very limited support within ACPO for many of the government's police reforms, it will be of interest to discover whether such fusion occurs among chief officers and LPAs in seeking to dilute some of the more centralising prescriptions emanating from Queen Anne's Gate. It might yet be a source of some irony if the continued centralising pressure from the Home Office generated alliances between police and police authorities which rejected the more overt forms of interference in operational policing which increasingly characterise current Home Office policy.

NOTES

1. Hoc. Deb., 23 March 1993, Cols.765–86.
2. Ibid., Col.767.
3. Interview local government officer (A1), 16 Oct. 1995.
4. K. Baker, Turbulent Years: My life in Politics (Faber, 1993).
5. Police Reform White Paper (HMSO, 1993).
6. Inquiry into Police Responsibilities & Rewards, Cm 2280.1 (HMSO, 1992).
7. Local Authority Survey of Police Authority Membership, 1994.
8. Interview local government officer (A2), 16 Oct. 1995.
9. See The Independent, 21 Jan. 1995.
10. Interview chairman of Warwickshire Police Authority, 15 April 1995.
11. IPCS Survey of independent members on the Police Authority, see also County News, April 1995.
12. IPCS Survey 1995, University of Portsmouth.
13. Interview with Dr Marie Dickie, Northamptonshire Police Authority, 12 July 1995.
14. Interview Cheshire Police Authority clerk.
15. Appointment of independent members, Home Office, 1993.
16. Interview Chief Constable 'B', 14 Sept. 1995.
17. Interview Chester, 13 Oct. 1995.
18. Ibid.
19. Graham Gordon, 'New Police Authorities – How New? How Local?', County News, July 1995.
20. Interview Chief Constable 'A', Oct. 1995.
21. Interview Chester, 13 Oct. 1995.
22. Ibid.
23. Ibid.
24. County News, July 1995.

25. Erica Stratta, *Policing*, Vol.6 (1990).
26. HMIC Report, Dorset Police (Home Office, 1995).
27. Interview, Chief Constable 'B', 14 Sept. 1995.
28. See Dr Marie Dickie, 'Locally Accountable Policing', *County News* (June 1995).
29. Interview, Chief Constable 'B', 14 Sept. 1995.
30. Interview, Chief Constable 'B', 14 Sept. 1995.
31. Chief Constable of Sussex, 16 Oct. 1995.
32. ACC Committee of LPAs Agenda Item 5, 'Role of HM Inspectorate of Constabulary', 7 Sept. 1995.
33. David Maclean, 'Consolidation and Community', *County News*, Oct. 1995.
34. Interview, Chief Constable 'B', 14 Sept. 1995.

Independence in Further Education: Managing the Change Process

INTRODUCTION

Over the last few years the government has introduced radical reforms of the education system. The 1988 Education Reform Act marked the beginning of a new configuration in the governance of local education services by introducing 'local management of schools' (LMS), open enrolment, and schools being allowed to 'opt out' of their Local Education Authorities (LEAs) and acquire grant maintained status. Reform has extended to the further and higher education (FHE) sector, focusing on education and vocational training and the growing partnership between business, industry and education. There has been a move towards centralisation of powers. The Education Reform Act 1988 shifted power over the curriculum from local government and schools to the centre, whilst giving delegated management to schools and colleges. Although in further education the link to central government is different, the government has not given any attention to the purposes or intervention of local government.

The Secretary of State for Education and Science, in a statement to the House of Commons on 21 March 1991, announced the government's intention to establish a new independent sector for post-16 education whereby funding would come from the government via a new statutory funding council (the FEFC). This new sector would include all maintained further education and sixth form colleges. The statement to the House made clear the Secretary of State's intention to take the sector out of local authority control. This announcement was followed by the publication of White Papers proposing legislation, *Education and Training for the 21st Century* (two volumes),[1] which dealt with further education and sixth form colleges. The FHE Act 1992 imposed a radically new institutional framework on further education (FE). Colleges were incorporated on 30 September 1992 and transferred from local authority control on 1 April 1993. The reforms have been based on a number of common themes; central government control of local expenditure, the market, individualism,

Jean Easton, Birmingham City Council

widening choice, improving quality of service, strengthening accountability and responsiveness, with the emphasis on increasing consumer power.

The purpose of this article is to investigate the organisational and management changes in post-16 education and training following the FHE Act 1992, focusing on how the newly incorporated colleges are managing the change process. It draws on research undertaken during 1993–94. The article looks at change from different perspectives. The primary perspective is the FE colleges in Birmingham and a neighbouring FE college in Solihull. The secondary perspective is the local authority, using Birmingham City Council as a case study.

The legislation has enormous implications for relationships between central and local government, and between the institutions and local authorities – and the communities they serve. New forms of accountability to the centre and within the locality are developing. This raises questions about what new relationships are developing and whether colleges operate in isolation as an island, or in a web of interconnectedness. In considering the nature of the changing relationships with the local authority the article also focuses on the changing role of the local authority. This will involve assessing whether the LEA's contribution to the system is confined to the 'residual duties' identified in the White Papers or whether the local authority can play a strategic role in the context of the enabling authority.

THE IMPACT OF THE LEGISLATION

The overall impact of the FHE Act was to eliminate the function of LEAs as the core providers of post-16 education. A timetable of events is summarised in Figure 1. This continues the trend established for vocational training with the establishment of Training and Enterprise Councils (TECs). [Fig 1 about here]

The key to these changes is a view that demographic changes, combined with industrial demands for a highly skilled workforce, require a more flexible educational establishment. Coupled with this is the government's commitment to raising standards and increasing choice. Establishing a new college sector for post-16 education and training was a major instrument for achieving these objectives. The government's intention was that colleges should have as much control as possible over their own affairs. Incorporation empowers them to make their own decisions and gives them freedom and flexibility to manage their academic and financial affairs within a national framework provided by the Further Education Funding Council (FEFC).

FIGURE 1
FURTHER AND HIGHER EDUCATION ACT 1992
IMPLEMENTATION TIMETABLE

May 1991	Publication of the Government's White Paper, 'Education and Training for the 21st Century' on which the FHE Act is based
November 1991	Publication of the Further and Higher Education Bill
February 1992	First circular (92/01) from the Further Education Funding Council Unit 'Preparing for Incorporation'
March 1992	Further and Higher Education Act passed
April 1992	Second circular (92/02) from the FEFC Unit, 'Preparing for Incorporation - Supplementary information'
	Publication of the Touche Ross Handbook of Guidance, 'Getting Your College Ready'
	Coopers & Lybrand Health and Safety Questionnaire
July 1992	Formal establishment of the FEFC . Members of FEFC regional committees announced
August 1992	Circular (92/11) from the FEFC Unit providing a framework for 'Preparing Strategic Plans'
September 1992	Transitional funding made available to colleges
	Establishment by the FEFC of arrangements for securing assessment of quality
30 Sept 1992	Incorporation Day, i.e. the incorporation of colleges as independent bodies separate from the LEA
January 1993	Announcements by the FEFC of the main allocations of recurrent funding to institutions for 1993/94
1 April 1993	Vesting Day
Further Education Corporations formally became independent institutions and staff transfer from LEA employment to employment by the corporation
September 1993	Circular (93/28) from the FEFC Unit, 'Assessing Achievement - Framework for Inspections in the FE Sector. Incorporating Amendments Following consultation'
February 1994	Colleges submit initial 'Stage 1' strategic plans to FEFC - extending over 16 month period from April 1993
July 1994	Colleges submit final 'Stage 2' strategic plans to FEFC

The Further Education Funding Council

The 'new' colleges are accountable to the FEFC. The FEFC was formally established in July 1992 and is a central part of the new structure. It is responsible for disbursing funds to the colleges and the oversight of the work of the sector, including quality assessment. The FEFC is responsible for the allocation of over £2 billion, formerly the responsibility of LEAs.

Regional Committees

The 'new' colleges' accountability to the FEFC is via a regional committee. The regional committees have responsibility for advising the FEFC on the 'sufficiency and suitability' of FE provision and on other FE issues, and undertake strategic planning. There are nine regions in England, the Birmingham and Solihull colleges being part of the West Midlands region. Each regional committee has about 12 members. Following lobbying from the TECs during the passage of the Bill each regional committee includes two representatives of local TEC interests. Thus the regional arms of the FEFC work closely with TECs, taking account of their views of local labour market needs and local vocational education and training provision.

In Birmingham some colleges have an additional accountability to the Birmingham TEC for work-related FE funding. Not only are these colleges subject to regional planning, but also to a Birmingham plan drawn up by the TEC. Therefore, for all colleges there are two levels of planning, via national and regional bodies. In the case of FE colleges, however, there will be an additional local level at the TEC. Clearly this is a bureaucratic structure of control.

The lack of such structures in the old Polytechnics and Colleges Funding Council system has meant that there was no convenient model for the government to draw on. In particular, the greater scale of the FE sector in terms of numbers of colleges, students and courses, as well as their diversity, could place a considerable responsibility on the regional level. In addition, there are the difficulties of co-ordination of 16–19 education following the removal of substantial parts of the school system from LEA control and the development of greater individual school autonomy for those still under the LEAs. The regional structure of the FEFC may well be best placed to provide this co-ordinating role, particularly since it has TEC representatives with local expertise (though, notably, none from the LEAs). However, unless they have some devolved executive funding power from the FEFC their role will be limited.

Removing FE colleges from LEA control with the establishment of a non-accountable funding council and regional committees also raises the question of what methods of accountability there will be to the local community. The legislation undermines the notion of local democratic principles since elected members do not sit on any of the committees. The education reforms have led to the formation of powerful national QUANGOS like the FEFC and the National Council for Vocational Qualifications. The governing body of each FE college is also being QUANGO-ised with greater business involvement. Unlike local government the meetings of QUANGOs are usually not open to the public.

Generally the basis on which decisions are made is hidden from public view and public scrutiny and, with a few exceptions, there is no requirement for the people involved to declare their interests. The ability of local communities through their elected representatives to influence not only the further education service but also a wide range of public services including health, housing, local economic development and urban regeneration has been removed, reducing the ability of local communities to govern themselves.

Government of FE Corporations

The FE corporations created by the Act are independent entities which are not owned, controlled or managed by the LEA. They are prevented from having formal LEA representatives on their governing bodies, although individuals who were previously LEA representatives have in some cases continued on governing bodies as co-opted 'independent' members.

The Department for Education's regulations on the government of further education corporations came into force on 30 September 1992. Shadow governing bodies operated from September 1992 to 1 April 1993 alongside the governors established under the 1988 Education Reform Act. The Instrument and Articles of Government in the final regulations were in some ways more rigid than the draft or the Act. For example, whereas the draft stipulated a range of size for governing bodies of 12–20 members, the actual regulations reduced the lower permitted size to ten. This was in spite of intense lobbying by various bodies arguing that 12 was too small for effective representation and accountability.

At their first meeting after 1 April 1993, the governors set the final size of the governing body and began the process of re-shaping the governing body by filling or not filling vacancies. In Birmingham the constitution of the governing bodies has not changed dramatically, since the local authority representatives have generally been co-opted in their industrial or commercial capacities and remain members at a 'personal level'. This keeps links with the local community. Local business community representation has brought different skills to the FE governing bodies. However, it has been argued that to date there is little evidence that it has brought skills which make things so much better.

A year after incorporation, Solihull College established a new committee or 'Foundation Board', similar to those in American Community Colleges. The Foundation Board runs alongside the college's governing body to advise on capital projects, secure funding for student welfare and promote the college's work. It comprises directors of local industry, elected members and the Chief Executive of Solihull Council. Incorporation has raised the issue of public accountability, with the establishment of non-elected committees and boards, and the removal of LEA representatives from governing bodies. This is an area which could attract further attention in the context of the wider debate on QUANGOs and probity in public bodies.

MANAGING ORGANISATIONAL CHANGE

Incorporation presented many challenges for the colleges in terms of organisational change. The main threat was whether the colleges would remain viable and survive, and within this context the colleges were faced with new demands and pressures requiring new organisational structures and systems. Across the board the colleges showed that they were prepared and adaptive to change although there are two isolated cases, at St Philip's Catholic Sixth Form College in Birmingham and at Derby Tertiary College, Wilmorton, where the Secretary of State for Education stepped in to investigate governors' mismanagement. Because colleges generally welcomed the legislation there was a sense of wanting to make it work. Many of the colleges described organisational change as being 'top down' and hierarchical. The legislation and the direction from the FEFC provided the driving force for change at the macro-level. At the college level, the governors and senior management teams moved and shaped those inputs.

Managing change is complex. Because of the extremely tight deadlines it was necessary for senior management teams to rush through the planning process to get to the outcome stage and become incorporated by 1 April 1993. Strong leadership and fast decision making were essential to meet the demands of the FEFC. Some colleges adopted more consultative methods than others. However, all of the colleges studied, with hindsight, would have wished for more time to concentrate on people's attitudes and values; particularly when they were feeling vulnerable and feared the impact of incorporation on their employment rights. One Principal commented that what the college had learned about organisation and development during incorporation was that 'it is people not structures that count' and that you can never communicate too much. However, the recent industrial action taken by lecturers at some colleges highlights the importance of two-way co-operation and negotiation.

In all the colleges studied particular effort was concentrated on communication and information in terms of circulating regular newsletters, bulletins and organising seminars for staff. The colleges had to adapt to major changes in new technology, to computerise financial systems and student records and registers. It was also necessary for each college to draw up a strategic plan which played an important part in the colleges' bids for resources.

The colleges are implementing innovative changes by extending the range of programmes to attract different client groups and to meet market demands. They have demonstrated that they are both flexible and entrepreneurial. For example, North Birmingham College is moving from a conventional traditional technical college towards community, leisure and learning facilities. Over time, it is envisaged that colleges will consolidate particular strengths and individual identities.

Continuing to try to change values and attitudes will be a long-term commitment for all the colleges. The colleges have identified a number of strategies for the future: strategic planning, improving management information systems and communications, reviewing their provision in line with quality standards and assessing growth possibilities. A number of Principals have highlighted the possibility of planning for expansion or mergers in view of the number of colleges in the West Midlands and the increased competition for students. There are also some interesting (although not unproblematical) developments in terms of 'franchising' where colleges are undertaking work with a partner, which may be another FE college, a higher education institution, schools or local industry.

RELATIONSHIPS

Incorporation has led to the development of a whole new network of relationships between the colleges and the local authority, other agencies and client groups and the wider community.

The legislation has shifted power away from the LEA to the incorporated college sector. These radical changes centre upon the government's view of local authorities as 'enablers' rather than direct service providers. Local authorities have lost a great deal of their functions and powers for education over the past few years: The increased devolution of funds to schools under local management arrangements, the opting for grant maintained status by some schools, the many changes in personnel and structure and now the loss of further and higher education as the post-16 education and training system is opened up to market forces. All these factors come together to demand a new definition of what the LEA can and should attain in the future.[2]

Incorporation raises a number of issues about what should be the future role of the LEA in a changing educational system and what should be its future relationship with the FE sector. The relationship has to change and must be seen in the context of the challenges facing local government. The challenges facing local government include capping and the general financial constraints affecting local authorities. Government policy has restricted the role of local authorities with the setting up of new non-elected bodies to carry out their former functions. The balance of power between central government, local government and education/training institutions has shifted as local authority powers transfer to the new FE sector. Thus legislation has created a fragmented system where colleges are the responsibility of the FEFC, non-vocational adult education is the responsibility of the LEA, and vocational training of young people is the responsibility of the TEC. This makes coherent planning impossible unless there are mechanisms for collaboration.

If the local authority simply reacts to the combination of trends described above it risks becoming marginal to the major events affecting the city and the vital concerns of its citizens. The local authority no longer has power or domination but is concerned to develop a new partnership with the FE sector. So what is the future role of the local authority? Can the local authority assert a new leadership role through influence? What are the issues for local authorities, and how can they develop the partnership with the FE colleges?

A Partnership Model – Birmingham City Council and the Incorporated Sector

The local authority role is not defined clearly in the legislation. The FHE Act did not include reference to any strategic role to be played by LEAs or local authorities in the new sector. However, in Birmingham there was general recognition that for a successful implementation it would be necessary for all key players to maintain a 'strategic partnership'. A structure setting out the Birmingham context is shown in Figure 2. However, a review of the relationships undertaken by the Forward Consultancy Division of Birmingham City Council suggested a general lack of trust between the main parties involved.[3] Disputes with the City Council over assets and treatment of college deficits were also identified as souring the emerging relationship.

The colleges argue that they want to operate in a strategic context although, given the basic competitive pressures, the city should not expect the colleges to speak 'with one voice' – unless it is possible for them to identify and agree clear benefits through a collaborative approach, for example, in promoting Birmingham or bidding for resources allocated on a regional basis such as the European Social Fund Objective 3. It is also important that dealings with individual colleges are 'transparent' and that colleges should be given equal opportunities to bid for any City Council training contracts or enter into partnerships around particular programmes or initiatives.

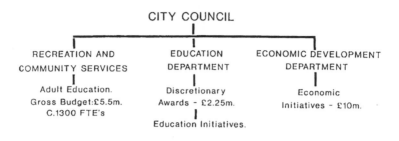

FIGURE 2
BIRMINGHAM CONTEXT

The City Council has a number of ways to exert leverage:

- A clear city-wide policy for post-16 education and training that relates to broader City Council economic and social objectives, for example with respect to economic regeneration
- A policy whose formulation the colleges can influence and 'buy into', as reflected in their own strategic planning activities.
- Participation or access to the city's strategic planning process; City Council-led activities with a European focus – for example, participation in the European funding strategies for the West Midlands and Birmingham, including the co-ordination of European bids; locally focused economic development initiatives – for example, local regeneration initiatives, City Challenge and integrated area initiatives; economic forecasting and local labour market analyses.

So far, the local authority services which the colleges have wished to use have been mixed, and include the continued use of services such as payroll, catering, cleaning and health and safety.

Birmingham City Council has established a structure to help keep links between the colleges and the local authority. A post-16 advisory group provides one mechanism for a continuing dialogue. It provides a single point of contact and a co-ordinated strategy and approach to cross-council policy on post-16 issues. Colleges will be encouraged to support the City Council's main objectives of equality, access, local area development, anti-poverty and so on. So, although the colleges are no longer part of the local authority, they can still contribute to an overall city strategy.

By working together it may be possible to increase the number of people who are actually benefiting from education. A new relationship can thus raise the achievement level for a number of client groups ranging from traditional school leavers to adults and people in employment. It is anticipated that in Birmingham the partnership with the FE colleges will develop over time. Many of the colleges have commented that the post-16 advisory group has provided a useful forum to discuss policy development and common areas for co-operation and collaboration.

However, although there is goodwill on both sides, the full potential of this group cannot be realised whilst it is subsumed by transitional issues such as college deficits and assets. A partnership is emerging but it is piecemeal, it lacks a framework, it is fragmented and is easily diverted by transitional issues. The local authority can create a forum to bring together the local players in support of overall strategic objectives and to ensure that there is a coherent pattern of provision. However, it could be argued that the colleges are currently operating more as desert islands than as a web of interconnectedness.

The colleges are generally responding to independence with vigour and enthusiasm, and feel that they are now in a better position to strive towards improving standards and efficiency and to encourage more people into FE. If they are successful in attracting students it will bring more money for education and training to the city than would have been possible for the local authority. The buildings and the college environments are improving because of the additional money for refurbishment. These are added-value dimensions which the colleges feel independence has brought. However, there is the danger that the pursuit of achievement by appointed boards could take priority over community values, highlighting the added-value which has been lost by the removal of local democratic processes.

An appointed body will not be directly linked to the community. The closure of a college will be determined by market forces and issues of closure and mergers have become sharper since incorporation. If a body has been appointed to improve efficiency, as the government proposed, then there is the danger that this objective will take priority over community values. The key question is whether an appointed system has the potential to add more value than a democratic one. It is too soon to evaluate outcomes and performance across all colleges following incorporation, but is an area which would be interesting to examine in, say, two to three years' time.

CONCLUSION

Despite the difficulties, the pressures and the vulnerability, most colleges were in favour of incorporation and became successfully incorporated by 1

April 1993. It is important to be explicit about why the colleges welcomed the legislation. They have felt that the LEA absorbed a disproportionate share of resources and have been frustrated by what they saw as a cumbersome administrative system. However, although incorporation empowers the colleges to manage their financial affairs independent of the LEA, they must now operate within the national/regional framework provided by the FEFC to meet national targets. The first and critical issue for colleges facing incorporation was successful management of the budget and the wider challenge facing colleges was the successful management of organisational change.

Incorporation required skills and understanding in the changing nature of information and communication, setting new goals and strategies, strategic planning, managing resources, the potential role of new technologies and implementing management information systems. The opportunities and threats of a more competitive environment require not just organisational but major cultural change in attitudes and values. The successful incorporated colleges, in the long run, will be those which, in addition to proper resource management, get the 'people' part of the organisation right.

The pace and complexity of the changes necessary to implement incorporation meant that it was not possible to involve staff as much as the college managements would have wanted. In the face of staff mistrust of changes in conditions of service, the future issue for colleges will be whether significant shifts in staff attitudes can be achieved in order to implement the full range of services demanded of colleges in the 1990s. Dealing with this will be a major challenge both nationally and for individual colleges.

The development of a new relationship between the local authority and colleges must be seen in the context of the wider changes and challenges facing local authorities as their role changes from direct service providers to 'enablers'. At the moment the new relationship is uneasy. The colleges and Birmingham City Council would both want the relationship to develop but transitional issues have caused difficulties.

The relationship needs to focus on what makes the relationship of value. How can the local authority meet the needs of the colleges? How can the colleges meet the needs and interests of the local authority? How well can the local authority co-ordinate strategic networks? There is nothing tried and tested in FE so it is necessary to look for new approaches in this area.

All colleges are engaged in some measure of collaboration, whether with the local authority, other colleges, or other agencies such as the TEC. The new networks are still embryonic but are developing a new confidence and maturity. FE has had no real national identity, but the FEFC does now give it national status. However, the FEFC may need to be more than a funding mechanism – it may need to make key strategic decisions about policy and future direction in the FE system. This raises the question of accountability. The total loss of local democratic accountability from FE was an issue of concern with incorporation. There is a growing need to consolidate a balance between appointed bodies and elected representation. Incorporation has brought with it a new business culture. However, there is a danger that the pursuit of 'business achievement' could take priority over community values, highlighting the added-value which has been lost by the removal of local democratic processes.

NOTES

This article is based on research undertaken whilst studying for a Master of Social Science degree at The University of Birmingham.

I would like to express my gratitude to the College Principals and Birmingham City Councillors and Officers interviewed as part of the research and whose professional knowledge and expertise has been invaluable in writing this article.

I would also like to thank Howard Davis of INLOGOV for his assistance with the preparation of this article and Chris Skelcher and Kathryn Riley for their help with the original research.

1. Department of Education and Science, *Education and Training for the 21st Century* (HMSO, 1991).
2. Audit Commission, *Losing an Empire, Finding a Role: The LEA of the Future* (HMSO, 1989).
3. Birmingham City Council Forward Consultancy Initiative, *Review of Organisational and Management Arrangements for Post 16 Education and Training* (Birmingham City Council, 1993).

Public Accountability in Today's Health Service

GUY B.J. DALY

INTRODUCTION

Structural changes within the reformed health service along with certain well publicised management failures have heightened interest in the arrangements for securing public accountability in the health service.[1] Government ministers and health service interests have seemingly been stung by the criticism of a lack of public accountability at a local level. It would seem that the democratic deficit can no longer be ignored.

It is no coincidence that the Department of Health has been concerning itself with how best to involve the public.[2] Virginia Bottomley, whilst she was still the Secretary of State for Health, had said that health authorities 'must actively encourage public participation in the decision making process'.[3] Whilst he was still Minister for Health, Brian Mawhinney was reported as having said that 'consultation with your local community is at the heart of your DHA's purchasing agenda ... to find out people's views about health services, and to take account of these views'.[4]

In examining the issues relating to the public accountability of today's health service, it will be argued in this article that the local choice dimension within the health service is increasing in significance.[5] The argument that the health service is (and always was) a national service will be challenged, as will the argument that public accountability does and should occur at the national level.

This in turn leads on to the consideration of how accountability in today's health service can best be achieved. The view expressed in this article is that it is no longer sustainable to oppose some form of democratic accountability that is both public and local. Whilst this view is not in itself entirely new, indeed the author and others have expressed similar ideas previously, its relevance has arguably never been more apposite.[6] The alternative of simply tinkering with the present system and yet leaving in place unaccountable appointees to continue to make decisions at a local level is no longer sustainable.

Guy Daly, Cheltenham and Gloucester College of Higher Education

There are a number of different models that could be employed in ensuring that local public accountability is achieved. The option to pass the responsibility over (some would say back) to local government is just one of the options that could be considered, along with the option of setting up directly elected, single-purpose health authorities. However, before considering the strengths and weaknesses of both of these, it is necessary to question the view that the health service is and always was a national service.

A WHOLLY *NATIONAL* SERVICE – A FLAWED VIEW OF HISTORY

Defenders of the present situation may give the impression that responsibility for the health service has been solely at the national level since 1948 and that any local government responsibility ended then. This is very far from the truth. Local authorities, through their direct responsibility for community health services and ambulance services, remained a crucial element of health service provision right up to 1974. It was only then that the health service moved fully into the world of appointed bodies. It is also important to note, as such initiatives as *The Health of the Nation* has recognised, that even today many local authority functions remain vital to health.[7]

However, the National Association of Health Authorities and Trusts (NAHAT), amongst others, has argued that recent reforms of the health service 'have not fundamentally altered the system of accountability'.[8] Indeed, Philip Hunt (NAHAT's director) has since stated that 'A plethora of mechanisms is already available to ensure that the NHS is accountable'.[9] Leaving aside the way in which this skates over the introduction of market systems of accountability, there is also a failure to acknowledge the removal of local authority representation from health authorities as part of the *Working for Patients* restructuring.[10]

This was no minor change. Local authority representation made up a third of the board memberships prior to this restructuring and provided a direct link to the elected government of our local communities. The removal of elected local representatives is a change which is increasingly being mirrored across a range of local public services and something which has been commented on extensively.[11]

A further significant change resulting from the *Working for Patients* restructuring was that health service managers became members of the authorities (as executive directors) for the first time. Placing executive officers onto the health authority boards as members has arguably confused their role as well as that of the non-executive members. Executive board members are now supposed to act both as managers and authority members. The roles are very different and potentially conflicting ones.

NAHAT argues that, 'From an NHS point of view the new boards have proved their worth'.[12] However, the structural changes within the health service have created a situation in which the limited public accountability of health authorities that was in place before the recent reforms has receded even further with the creation of purchasing authorities, provider trusts and general practice fundholders (GPFHs).

The contention of this article is that those responsible for health services at the local level must be publicly accountable at the local level. As Stewart and Davis have said, 'those who exercise public power should be accountable to those on whose behalf they exercise that power. This requires both, a means of holding to account; and the giving of an account'.[13] If they act at a local level, they should be publicly accountable to local people.

Whereas it is clear that local councils are accountable to local people who can, if necessary, remove them via the electoral process, there is no way in which local people can hold the members of appointed boards to account. The boards can follow policies to which local people object, they can provide inadequate services for local people, they can even abuse their position, and there is nothing that local people can do directly to remove them. Regrettably, the health services in the West Midlands and Wessex have provided ample illumination of a number of these issues.[14]

The principle of public accountability needs to be embedded within public services but is currently seriously lacking and is being eroded at an ever-increasing rate, including within the reformed health service. Or, as Stewart has put it, 'Public institutions are justified by their basis in public accountability. Without that they are not rational in a democratic society'.[15]

HEALTH SERVICE ACCOUNTABILITY

Public accountability in the health service is far from adequate. The health authority board members are government appointments and as such are not locally accountable. Rather, the limited accountability that is available is through a long and uncertain line of accountability to the government's Secretary of State for Health. The minister is then accountable to parliament, which is in turn accountable to the electorate. The abolition of the regional health authorities (RHAs) and the amalgamation of district health authorities (DHAs) with family health service authorities (FHSAs) from April 1996 does not make the appointment of members more transparent or open. Hennessy has referred to this generally as the development of 'the alibi society – "Don't bother me, I'm only the Secretary of State"'.[16] It is the confused and tangled web of appointments, and hence accountability, that leads to this situation.

The health service is structured on the principle of sets of appointees watching, cajoling and interacting with other sets of appointees. It is difficult, therefore, to pinpoint the locus of power and authority within such a system. One is unsure as to whether one appointee has greater status than another. Crucially, it is extremely difficult to locate the point of access for members of the public.

The burden of accountability on ministers increases as effective local accountability decreases. Furthermore, health authorities, trusts and general practice fundholders (GPFHs) are not subject to the rigorous processes of public accountability that apply to elected local councils. For example, many hold their meetings in private. For all the attempts at administrative and managerial restructuring there has been little or no energy devoted to tackling the lack of an effective political voice for affected communities – unless one accepts William Waldegrave's argument that accountability has been ensured by the recent reforms, in that the newly reformed service is more responsive to the customer/consumer. He argued that this, the mimicking of the market, allows for a more responsive (and therefore accountable) service.[17]

Hunt has argued that the health service is a national service and that 'proper accountability is being exercised', at least at the national level. Therefore for some there would seem to be nothing drastically wrong with current mechanisms for accountability?'[18] This line of argument essentially takes the view that because the health service is a national, rather than a local service, it therefore needs to be steered by national policy and decision making. Accountability is ensured via accountability to parliament along with other supporting mechanisms: 'The Secretary of State is accountable to Parliament ... Parliamentary accountability is reinforced by the work of the Select Committee on Health and the Public Accounts Committee ... [which is] supported by the National Audit Office.'[19] At the same time, it is argued, the health service reforms have allowed for a better managed, more efficient decision-making service to be operated. Indeed, *Working for Patients* argued that what was needed were structures which could:

> handle the complex managerial and contractual issues that the new system demands, and that [for] health authorities ... to discharge their new responsibilities in a business-like way they need to be smaller and to bring together executive and non-executive members to provide a single focus for effective decision making.[20]

In contrast, locally accountable services would lead to an over-bureaucratised and stifling situation.

Perhaps managerial improvements have occurred and certainly codes of practice on openness have been drawn up since the events which lead to the

1994 House of Commons Public Accounts Committee commenting that management 'failings' represented 'a departure from the standards of public conduct which have mainly been established during the past 140 years'.[21] Even so, such improvements have not gone far enough.[22] Local public accountability is still absent.

Public accountability for the health service at a local level is required. Whilst not wishing to deny the desirability of a national framework, it must be accepted that ever since its inception there have been discrepancies over the nature and level of health care provision, whether between regions or more locally. The recent debate about inequities in the new funding formula is just one of the more recent examples of disagreements over inequitable levels of funding between health authorities.[23]

Health authorities are doing more than simply managing health services at a local level. Rather, local health authorities are daily making decisions about local needs and local priorities. National policy considerations such as *priority setting* demonstrate that they are encouraged to do so.[24] At the same time, evidence of actual choices being made at the local level continues to be produced; the case of Jaymee Bowen ('Child B') being perhaps the most notable recent example.[25] As Ham has said, 'responsibility for setting priorities hinges crucially on the decisions taken by health authorities locally on the interpretation of national policies – as the Cambridge case [Jaymee Bowen – 'Child B'] shows well'.[26]

Furthermore, the new health service is all about purchasers making local choices. Indeed, in many ways that is why they are there. (If they are not making local choices then perhaps they too should be abolished along with the RHAs and be replaced by local offices of the NHS executive at the district level.) The health authorities and GPFHs are choosing what to purchase, how much and from whom. Essentially local choices are being made; indeed this has been acknowledged by, amongst others, Ron Zimmern (the Director of Public Heath for Cambridge Health Commission – the health authority responsible for not funding 'Child B's' treatment).[27]

Local public accountability in the health service is therefore both appropriate and necessary. As Stewart has said more generally, 'Accountability at [the] local level is appropriate where services are delivered at local level and where choices are made at that level about the nature and level of services'.[28] Without it there is an overburdening at the national level. Ministers have been reluctant to accept personal responsibility for failings at a regional or local level, for example in the West Midlands and Wessex RHAs. Instead, if anyone, local appointees have 'carried the can'. For accountability to reside at national level, then, one would reasonably expect the ministers concerned to take full responsibility for the actions of their non-elected appointees in the health authorities and trust units. This has not happened.

Interrelated with this is the change in the nature of the provider units. They are now, as health service trusts, literally in the business of seeking out contracts. The new trusts may be giving preferential treatment to GPFHs. At the same time that this is happening, trusts may be winning contracts to supply services outside their locality and conversely may be losing out on contracts with their local purchasers (a recent example of this being the winning of a contract by a trust in Burton-on-Trent for community nursing in Cardiff).[29] Whereas in the past district hospitals and community services would have provided almost everything for the local community, they may no longer be contracted to do so. Indeed, the existence and viability of local provider units and trusts is being threatened, irrespective of the opposition of local people to such reconfigurations of their local health services.

LOCAL CHOICES

Local choices have always been made in the health service. As Ham has said, 'This responsibility is not new to district health authorities, who have long been in the position of having to determine local priorities'.[30] With the development of the local purchasing role this is now even more the case. Health authorities are no longer directly responsible for providing health services so that, for Ham,

> What is different is that, as purchasers, district health authorities may be able to take decisions which depend less on the demands of providers than they have in the past. In so doing, district health authorities should be able to place greater weight on other factors, such as *the views of local people* and evidence on the cost effectiveness of different services.[31] [emphasis added]

However, democratic accountability for such choices does not exist locally. Instead, it theoretically returns to the door of the appropriate minister. But, as has already been said, they are all too reluctant to accept responsibility for their appointees' local decisions.

For some, it may be that too much democratic involvement could be to the detriment of the smooth running of the service since the involvement of elected local representatives may lead to a replication of the perceived disadvantages of local government, namely: 'a common characteristic of local government is one of "committee-itis" and stultifying bureaucracy',[32] which would get in the way of the smooth management of the health service, especially when the service is in the midst of making difficult decisions over acute services. 'There is no guarantee that a local democratic process could help with the massive challenge posed by the major reconfiguration of acute services now taking place.'[33]

But this is precisely why a locally accountable service is needed, to ensure that those difficult decisions are taken in consultation with the community affected. This does not mean that difficult decisions cannot and will not be taken but rather that an intrinsic part of the process is that decision making needs to be taken openly and with the facility to call the decision makers to account.

The assertion that difficult decisions are fudged or obfuscated by local politicians is not credible. Local politicians have to close schools, make unpopular planning decisions, shut swimming baths; often in spite of local opposition. However, in these cases the community does have the opportunity of challenging, influencing and ultimately of removing the decision makers from office if they disagree with them.

It may well be easier for difficult decisions to be made behind closed doors with the community unable to call the decision makers to account. But ends do not justify means. Indeed, sometimes it may make for a more difficult life to have open and accountable decision making, but this more arduous journey makes the end more legitimate.

POSSIBLE OPTIONS: LOCAL AUTHORITY CONTROL OR DIRECTLY ELECTED HEALTH AUTHORITIES

Local democratic governance could be achieved by giving local authorities the responsibility for the commissioning of health services and this is something for which a number of people have argued.[34] Local authorities are responsible for commissioning social care and there is some logic to there being one body responsible for commissioning both health and social care. As NAHAT has said, 'It is possible to see how in the future the division between health and social care will become increasingly blurred'.[35]

Local authorities are also playing a key role in the attempts to improve the health of their localities. The *Health of the Nation* initiative is the latest to recognise the vital role that local authorities must play in ensuring that 'healthy alliances' take place.[36] Health gain is not going to be achieved simply by initiatives undertaken by health services. It is more likely to occur in the future, as it has in the past, with healthy alliances across a number of local public services, particularly those that are the responsibility of local authorities – environmental health, leisure, education, housing and social services. As David Knowles has said, 'It is increasingly accepted that improvements to areas such as housing and environmental services are often the most significant way to achieve better health'.[37] The prospect of the responsibility for the running of health services returning to the local *political* arena is feared by some. But it is necessary to recognise that health services have always been political. Whenever choices are being made regarding levels of resourcing and levels of service, value judgements are being made. Presently, these choices are being made at a local level by locally unaccountable appointees.

The argument that it is inappropriate for local government to be responsible for a national service such as health is something that this article has demonstrated not to be the case. Local choices are being made, albeit within a nationally steered framework. Differences over levels of service, types of treatments available and eligibility can already be seen between health authorities.

It would be both possible and legitimate for health services to come under the responsibility of local government. Decisions would have to be made, though, about the current lack of co-terminosity between health authority and local authority boundaries. Secondly, adequate resources would have to flow to local government with the transfer of responsibility for health services.

There is, however, another option. The directly elected health authority is frequently ignored as a policy option. A somewhat disingenuous leap is often made by opponents of local democratic accountability in the health service in that the arguments for democratic local accountability are invariably equated with arguments for local government control of the health service.[38] Whilst there are indeed strong arguments for expanding local government's responsibilities, the arguments for democratic public accountability of the health service at the local level cannot be dismissed simply by arguing against local government control. Democratic local control of the health service can exist quite separately from local government and a major omission is often made by not even considering this approach.

The creation of directly elected local health authorities is one way of avoiding many of the concerns levelled against local authority control of health services as well as at the same time offering the opportunity for a real and focused debate on local health priorities. The 'local state' has already become fragmented, whereby there is now an emphasis on partnership between the various separate local players. It would be quite possible for locally elected health authorities to build 'healthy alliances' with the appropriate partners, including the local authority. A directly elected local health authority's sole concern would be for commissioning health services. This in turn would ensure that there was no opportunity for diverting resources away from health.

Elected health authorities would not necessarily lead to the party politicisation of health at a local level. Representatives of health professionals and other health staff, user-representatives, individual members of the public, members of the local CHCs could all stand for election. An advantage of directly elected health authorities as opposed to the local government option is that people would be able to vote specifically on health issues. There would be no necessity to weigh up the strengths of a candidate's position on a number of issues.

The criticism that it would be inappropriate to have local accountability for health services which are financed in the main from national funds is not a sufficient argument against change. Local government presently finds itself in such a position, yet few would seriously argue that elected local government should be completely abolished.

TINKERING WITH THE CURRENT SYSTEM

There is a view that, rather than creating even more upheaval in an otherwise basically sound health service, all that needs to be done is to make a number of improvements to the current situation. In this vein, one has witnessed the 'Nolan' recommendations concerning appointments to non-elected public bodies (including health authorities) and, for its part, the Labour Party's proposals to revamp health authorities (which would be renamed 'supervisory boards') by including local community representatives along with patients' groups and health professionals.[39] In addition, the Department of Health has also emphasised the need to involve local voices and has also implemented, amongst other codes, a code of practice on openness in the NHS for health authorities, trusts and GPFHs.[40] There have also been calls to strengthen the role of community health councils. However, none of these initiatives tackle the problem of the lack of democratic accountability at the local level. They merely tinker with a flawed situation.

The 'Nolan' recommendation to set up an independent commissioner to oversee the appointment of members of QUANGOs, and the desire for members to be more representative of their communities is surely an improvement on the present situation.[41] The Labour Party's proposals to set up supervisory boards of non-executive directors representing the local community are also an improvement but remain inadequate for the reason that there is a continuing failure to address the local democratic deficit.[42] Even if the methods used to appoint future non-executive board members are seen to be more open, and even if the members are more representative in a demographic sense, the need for democratic accountability at the local level remains.

The recent emphasis on health services involving local voices, whether through the use of locality purchasing, surveys and opinion polls, focus groups, standing panels and citizens' juries, is to be welcomed as a way of informing decision making and decision makers.[43] However, there is a risk that what is created is an even less accountable situation in which unaccountable health authority members end up listening to individuals who represent no one: 'the unaccountable in pursuit of the uninformed'.[44]

Community Health Councils (CHCs) also have a role to play. However, the existence of CHCs does nothing to ensure that the democratic deficit at a local level is addressed. Their role is one of local watchdog. Anyway, it can be argued that CHCs themselves are problematical because of the difficult juggling act that they have to perform. They have to strike a balance between, on the one hand, not being too confrontational with their local purchasers and providers, in which case they would risk losing the power to influence, and, on the other, not becoming so cosy that they lose their independent voice. Indeed, as CHCs are re-established with the restructuring of health authorities in April 1996 they may be further compromised. Local health authorities will be responsible for holding contracts of employment for CHC staff and hold the leases or deeds for CHCs' premises.[45] As the Institute of Health Services Management and the Association of Community Health Councils for England said in a joint report, 'There are concerns that the CHC whose health authority holds the contract for all CHCs in that region might be vulnerable to particular pressure from that health authority'.[46] Measures such as codes of conduct and involving local people, along with a continuing role for CHCs, are useful additions to other mechanisms in ensuring that health authorities operate in an open manner. But, no amount of tinkering with the present arrangements can act as an adequate substitution for local democratic accountability.

CONCLUSION

In terms of its responsiveness to local needs and opinions the health service is deeply flawed. Public accountability for health services should involve more than simply allowing for the periodic questioning of the appropriate Secretary of State. Such a process does not allow the public to hold those responsible to account when hospitals are being closed, bed numbers are being reduced, specific waiting times being shortened or extended irrespective of the seriousness of the clinical condition, budgets exhausted before the end of the financial period. By choosing one option a health authority is denying another. Such decisions affect the health care that the public hopes to receive. These are not management but governmental decisions.

Those responsible for decisions must be held to account for their actions on a regular basis and in a public arena. Where decisions are about *local* needs and *local* priorities, this should be at the local level. The inescapable conclusion must be that there can be no effective substitute for the local ballot box. There are a number of ways that this could be achieved, such as through local government being given the responsibility or through the creation of directly elected health authorities.

Accountability at national level for local decision making is inappropriate and no longer sustainable. Political decisions over the allocation of resources are made by members largely unknown and inaccessible to the majority of us. Tinkering with the system is no longer a credible response.

NOTES

1. See, for instance, House of Commons Public Accounts Committee, *The Proper Conduct of Public Business* (HMSO, January 1994).
2. NHS Management Executive, 'Local Voices: The Views of Local People in Purchasing for Health' (1992).
3. Quoted in *Financial Times*, 26 Oct. 1993.
4. Cited in P.Hunt, 'Accountability in the National Health Service', *Parliamentary Affairs*, Vol.48, No.2 (1995), p.298.
5. The argument presented is a development of those contained in the mimeo: G. Daly and H. Davis, *Public Accountability in Today's Health Service* (University of Birmingham, 1995).
6. See, for instance, G. Daly and H. Davis, 'Give Us Democracy', *Nursing Times*, Vol.84, No.23 (1988), p.62.
7. Department of Health, *The Health of the Nation: A Strategy for Health in England*, Cm.1986 (HMSO, 1992).
8. National Association of Health Authorities and Trusts, 'Securing Effective Public Accountability in the NHS', NAHAT (1993), p.2.
9. P. Hunt, 'Accountability in the National Health Service', *Parliamentary Affairs*, Vol.48, No.2 (1995), p.301.
10. Department of Health, *Working for Patients*, Cmd.555 (HMSO, 1989).
11. See, for instance, H. Davis and J. Stewart, *The Growth of Government by Appointment: Implications for Local Democracy* (Local Government Management Board, 1993).
12. National Association of Health Authorities and Trusts, 'Securing Effective Public Accountability in the NHS', NAHAT (1993), p.5.
13. J. Stewart and H. Davis, 'A New Agenda For Local Governance', *Public Money and Management* (Oct.–Dec. 1994), p.32.
14. House of Commons Public Accounts Committee, op. cit., annex 2.
15. J. Stewart, 'Defending Public Accountability, *DEMOS*, Winter Quarterly (1993).
16. *The Observer*, 30 Jan. 1994.
17. W. Waldegrave, *The Reality of Reform and Accountability in Today's Public Service* (CIPFA, 1993).
18. P. Hunt, op. cit., p.303.
19. Ibid., pp.301–2.
20. Department of Health, *Working for Patients*, Cmd.555 (HMSO, 1989).
21. House of Commons Public Accounts Committee, op. cit., para.1.
22. H. Davis and G. Daly, 'Codes Of Conduct Are Not Enough', *The IHSM Network*, Vol.2, No.4 (1995), p.3.
23. 'Study Claims Inner Cities Policy is Unjust', *Health Service Journal* Vol.105, No.5477 (2 Nov. 1995), p.6; J. Hacking, 'For Richer, For Poorer', *Health Service Journal*, Vol.105, No.5463 (27 July 1995), pp.22–4.
24. House of Commons Health Committee, *Priority Setting in the NHS: Purchasing. First*

Report Sessions 1994–95 (HMSO, 1995); Department of Health, *Government Response to the First Report from the Health Committee Session 1994–5*, Cm.2826 (HMSO, 1995).
25. J. Jones, 'Should We Save Only The Young?', *The Observer*, 29 Oct. 1995.
26. C. Ham, 'Health Care Rationing', *British Medical Journal*, Vol.310 (1995), p.1484.
27. R. Zimmern, 'Insufficient to Simply be Efficient', *Health Service Journal*, Vol.105, No.5467 (1995), p.19.
28. J. Stewart, 'Defending Public Accountability', *DEMOS* (Winter 1993).
29. 'Welsh GPs to Move Contract to England', *Health Service Journal*, Vol.105, No.5480 (1995), p.4.
30. C. Ham, 'Priority Setting in the NHS: Reports from Six Districts', *British Medical Journal*, Vol.307 (14 Aug. 1993), p.435.
31. Ibid.
32. P. Hunt, 'Still Open To Question', *Health Service Journal*, Vol.103, No.5383 (1993), p.21.
33. Ibid.
34. See, for instance, N. Willmore, 'Hands On Health', *Local Government Chronicle*, 7 Jan. 1994, p.10.
35 National Association of Health Authorities and Trusts, op. cit.
36. Department of Health, *The Health of the Nation*.
37. In N. Willmore, op. cit.
38. See, for instance, P. Hunt, op. cit.
39. *Standards in Public Life: First Report of the Committee on Standards in Public Life*, Cm.2850–51 (HMSO, 1995); The Labour Party, *Renewing the NHS* (1995).
40. NHS Management Executive, op. cit.; NHS Executive, *Code of Practice on Openness in the NHS* (1995).
41. *Standards in Public Life*.
42. The Labour Party, *Renewing the NHS* (1995), p.20.
43. NHS Management Executive, op. cit.
44. N. Pfeffer and A. Pollack, 'Public Opinion and the NHS: The Unaccountable in Pursuit of the Uninformed', *British Medical Journal*, 25 Sept. 1993.
45. NHS Executive, *Report of the Working Group on the Implications of the Change in the Establishing Arrangements for Community Health Councils* (1995)
46. IHSM, 'Back from the Margins' (1995).

The Indirectly Elected World of Local Government

STEVE LEACH

In the debate about the fragmentation of local government and the gradual transfer of responsibilities from elected local authorities to appointed single-purpose bodies, joint authorities occupy an interesting intermediate position. With the exception of the former police authorities, joint boards (and joint committees) are composed entirely of elected councillors. However, the body to which these councillors have been directly elected is not the joint board itself, but rather to a district council or London borough which has then nominated them to sit on the body concerned. They are *appointees,* just as they would be on any other external organisation to which they were appointed.

These distinctions may sound semantic, but they are not. In particular, it is fallacious to argue that a joint body is accountable in the same way that a local authority is just because it is composed of councillors. As John Stewart[1] has rightly pointed out, 'Representativeness is not a little package you can carry around with you and give to any organisation to which the council appoints you. A councillor on a Joint Board is not elected to that Board. He is appointed to it'. This concern about the accountability of joint authorities was echoed in the Department of the Environment's policy guidance to the Local Government Commission.[2] 'Statutory joint authorities may be needed for some services but they do not benefit from the same accountability as individual authorities and a structure which does not require them is to be preferred.'

The issues of the accountability of joint bodies, which are in many respects different from the issues of accountability in non-elected local bodies, are discussed in the next section. But accountability is by no means the only important aspect of the operation of joint bodies which merits examination. The role of the chair, the relationship between members and the professional and administrative officers advising and servicing the joint body, and the scope for co-ordination between the joint body's activities and other related service areas are also matters of concern.

Before this agenda is discussed, however, it is necessary to clarify the

Steve Leach, De Montfort University, Leicester

terminology associated with joint activities. The range of options in relation to joint activity at the political level[3] is greater than the familiar distinction between a joint board[4] and a joint committee[5] would imply. Joint arrangements between two or more authorities may involve any of the following forms:

1. A joint authority which is legally a separate entity – the joint board.
2. An 'executive joint committee' to which decision-making and budget allocation powers have been delegated by a group of authorities for a specified time period and with a specified period of notice required for authorities wishing to resign their membership.
3. A 'consultative joint committee', which can only make decisions if all its members agree, with subsequent ratification by the parent authorities normally required.
4. Informal political arrangements to deal with a specific non-recurrent problem.

Examples of each of these forms of joint arrangements can be identified in the post-abolition machinery set up in 1986 in the six metropolitan counties. Greater Manchester, for example, had (*inter alia*) joint boards for police, fire, passenger transport and waste disposal, executive joint committees for superannuation and certain aspects of planning and countryside issues and highways respectively, and a consultative joint committee (AGMA), made up of the leaders of each of the ten districts concerned, to discuss issues of county-wide concern. When in 1986–88 the strategic guidance for the unitary development plans was being drawn up, *ad hoc* informal meetings of the chairs of planning committees were instituted in West Yorkshire and in the other metropolitan counties which did not operate a more formalised Joint Planning Committee. Although much of the recent interest in joint arrangements has been stimulated by the abolition of the Greater London Council (GLC) and the six metropolitan county councils, there are several relevant examples from the non-metropolitan areas – for example the unique Norfolk Joint Museums Committee[6] and the joint committees and boards which supervise the operation of our national parks.[7]

For the purposes of this article, emphasis is placed on joint boards and executive joint committees with delegated power. Although the former are explicitly single-purpose bodies, whilst the latter are not, the two forms of joint arrangement behave in practice in similar ways, and will raise similar issues for accountability, member–officer relations, and so on. Consultative joint committees and *ad hoc* political arrangements do not raise the same issues of principle in relation to accountability, as the Department of the Environment's policy guidance to the Local Government Commission recognises.[8] Indeed the recent reorganisations of local government in

England, Wales and Scotland have brought the issue of the accountability of joint arrangements back onto the public agenda; and following a review of the experience of joint arrangements in the metropolitan counties, the final section of this article examines the current reorganisations from this perspective.

THE EXPERIENCE OF JOINT ARRANGEMENTS IN THE METROPOLITAN COUNTIES

Joint boards and executive joint committees are an important feature in the governance arrangements of each of the six metropolitan counties. In each area there are joint boards for fire and passenger transport. In Greater Manchester and Merseyside there are joint boards for waste disposal. Joint committees with executive powers operate in all six counties to manage the county-wide superannuation fund. Joint committees with executive powers and allocated budgets supervise trading standards and waste disposal in West Yorkshire, and the river valleys scheme in Greater Manchester. There are a range of other more minor functions dealt with in this way. Before the recent creation of free-standing police authorities joint boards also existed for police.[9] Thus it cannot reasonably be claimed that executive joint machinery is a limited and marginal feature of the local government operations in these areas. Joint action covers a wide range of functions and involves considerable expenditure.[10]

There are three important ways in which services provided by joint boards and executive joint committees differ from those provided by individual local authorities. Firstly, the direct accountability link is broken, and questions then emerge about the sense in which joint boards are accountable. Secondly, because they are detached from the normal run of local authority business, the relationship between members and officers changes, and the position of the chair is highlighted. Thirdly, for a similar reason the scope for co-ordination between the service provided by the joint board and related services is more problematical than if all the services involved were run by the same authority. Each issue will be considered in turn.

ACCOUNTABILITY ISSUES

The normal conception of political accountability is one which is congruent with the notion of representative democracy.

> Representative democracy (in the party-dominated local government system ...) involves a system whereby each political party contesting

seats at an election makes a public statement (typically in the form of a manifesto) as to what it will seek to achieve if it obtains a majority of council seats at the election (or what it will argue or press for if it does not) ... Once elected, the councillor is expected to use his or her judgement ... He or she is a *representative*, not a delegate. Thus in a system of representative democracy, the link between a clear party election statement and the capacity to put that statement into operation is crucial.[11]

The system of government which now operates in the metropolitan counties – in so far as it involves joint boards and executive joint committees – by definition and in practice lacks the capacity for political accountability based on this concept of representative democracy, because,

councillors are not *elected* as members of joint bodies, they are *appointed* by district councils to serve on them. This does not mean, ... that there is no basis upon which local electors in district elections can be presented with manifesto material on joint authorities. What it does mean is that the direct link between a manifesto promise ... and the capacity to carry out that promise cannot exist in relation to activities which are the responsibility of a joint ... body.[12]

But there are alternative interpretations of accountability which may be applicable to joint bodies and provide a rationale for their operation. Gyford *et al.*[13] identify four different conceptions of democracy, which provide the basis for alternative conceptions of accountability (see Figure 1).

FIGURE 1
FOUR VARIANTS OF DEMOCRACY

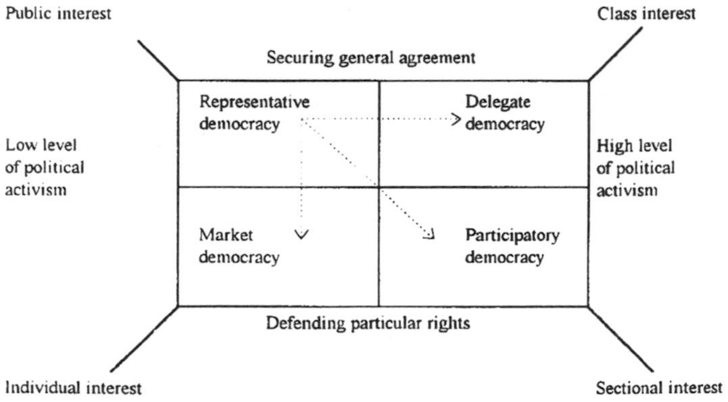

Source: Reproduced from Gyford *et al.*, op. cit., p. 346.

Neither market democracy/accountability nor participatory democracy/ accountability is particularly appropriate to the functions which are the responsibility of the joint bodies in the metropolitan counties. The relevance of 'delegate democracy' is, however, worth exploring in more detail. Delegate democracy in the model depicted above would normally be associated with the internal processes of political parties, that is, the right of a local party to mandate councillors from that party who sit on a joint body to follow a particular line. However the Conservative government developed an alternative conception of delegate accountability – with an element, one suspects, of *post-hoc* rationalisation – based on district councils rather than local parties. 'Being made up of elected councillors appointed by the borough and district councils, the new joint authorities will be part of the local government system in these areas.'[14]

There are thus two potential tests of the effectiveness of delegate democracy,

> Firstly, if there existed strong and active county parties to which members of the joint bodies viewed themselves as being accountable, with effective mandating and reporting back mechanisms operating between the county parties and joint board members, then this would meet the main accountability criteria associated with delegate democracy. Or, taking the government's standpoint, if similar mechanisms operated effectively between the districts themselves and joint board members, then the joint bodies could be argued to be operating accountably in terms of delegate democracy.[15]

Any other form of mandating (or reporting back) – for example of the chair of a joint board by a group of district Labour leaders, either constituted formally as a co-ordinating committee or meeting more informally – whatever other purpose it may serve, cannot justifiably be construed as an example of 'delegate democracy' in action. Indeed it is much more likely to constitute an example of the informal use of oligarchic power!

What has been the reality? As far as the Labour Party is concerned (and the Labour Party has been the dominant political force in metropolitan counties and on joint boards and committees since 1986) there was already established a piece of party machinery which could have provided an accountability link for Labour members of such bodies. The Metropolitan Labour Parties (MLPs) were continued beyond 1986, with specific responsibilities for joint board policy issues (their responsibility in relation to joint committee activities was more contested by district parties and district council Labour groups). There were and are, however, no parallel mechanisms as far as the Conservative or Liberal Democrat Parties are concerned. For these parties, delegate democracy in the 'local party' sense is not possible because local parties do not exist at this level.

In practice, even for the Labour Party, the arguments that delegate democracy provides a satisfactory basis for accountability, cannot be sustained.[16] Whatever the Labour Party rulebook said, in reality MLPs were non-operational after 1986 in four of the six metropolitan counties. Only in West Yorkshire and Greater Manchester did MLPs meet on a regular basis between 1986 and 1990. They were not wholly uninfluential in relation to Labour group policy on joint boards. In some cases Labour joint board chairs played an active part in MLP deliberations and participated in the drawing up of policy statements for the joint boards' remit. Sometimes District Labour Parties included MLP policy statements on joint board functions in their local election manifestos. But such examples were rare, and, furthermore, if a Labour joint board chair did not participate in MLP meetings, or if he or she was not happy with the policy advice which emerged, such advice was invariably ignored. The problem for MLPs was that they had no real sanctions – disciplinary or otherwise. In particular, as there was no equivalence between the MLP and a directly elected body, there was little that could be done to influence the re-selection of councillors (a more potent weapon for District Labour Parties). As a result MLPs only influenced Labour joint board members if they wished to be influenced, which hardly comprises a satisfactory form of delegate democracy/ accountability. In 1995 the MLPs were discontinued by the Labour Party and thus the potentiality for delegate democracy, in this sense, no longer exists for any of the major parties.

What of the government's novel conception of delegate democracy via district councils referred to above? Has this been effective? Do districts 'control' joint bodies by mandating their members to operate in ways which reflect districts' priorities in relation to joint board issues? The answer is that, with only a handful of occasional exceptions, they do not.

The first reason for this is that, given the dominance of (relatively adversarial) party politics in most districts, it would be quite unrealistic to expect an opposition member to accept a mandate from the majority party. It is inconceivable that a Conservative joint board member would take seriously an attempt by the controlling Labour group to mandate him (or her), whatever formal motion was passed at a committee or sub-committee, unless he or she happened to agree with it. Things just do not work like that. And if the controlling Labour group decided to remove the recalcitrant Conservative councillor from the joint board for not accepting the mandate they would have to replace him or her with another Conservative councillor who would presumably be just as likely to behave in the same way. The only conceivable mandating link would be of majority party joint board members, by the majority party in the council, acting either through the formal committee machinery, or informally.

As Leach[17] concluded, the accountability processes of joint boards are seriously flawed.

> With very few exceptions, [joint board] members were left unconstrained to operate as they felt appropriate on such bodies. In practice, this meant that any briefings required by councillors to enable them to develop a view tended to come from officers responsible for the joint board services (e.g, chief constable, chief fire officer, PTE director-general) or occasionally from someone from the lead authority: and any pressure to adopt a particular policy line tended to come from the party group on the joint board or occasionally a metropolitan party (where it existed).
>
> ... on any criteria of accountability, based on any conception of democracy, there has been since abolition a marked reduction in accountability ... in the metropolitan areas, where for the ex-county council functions, representative democracy has been eroded, and apparently replaced (or supplemented) by a system of delegate democracy (linking district councils and joint authorities). In practice however the new system does not operate in this way at all and joint board members are not held accountable by districts nor, it would appear, by anyone else. The messiness and unsatisfactoriness of the system, in accountability terms, is quite apparent.[18]

MEMBER–OFFICER RELATIONSHIPS

In most local authorities, the formal activity of a particular committee is typically supplemented by a good deal of informal activity amongst its members in relation to its agendas and responsibilities. The members of that committee are likely to meet informally to discuss specific issues during the normal course of their activities within the authority. They are likely to seek information from the officers involved in the business of the committee. If the authority has an active central policy unit, or has appointed post-Widdicombe 'political advisers', then councillors may also be able to obtain an alternative briefing from that provided by the chief officer whose departmental responsibilities the committee shadows. In this way a healthy and informed debate can take place, if not in the committee itself, at least amongst the majority party group members who are represented on the committee. The possibility exists for individual members to lobby other members informally to try to create a critical mass in support of a particular view (which may in certain circumstances be a view which is different from that of the committee chair). In other words, there exists a rich set of informal channels for informing oneself about committee agenda issues and seeking to persuade others of one's views. These channels are, of course, not always utilised; but they do exist.

In relation to joint board activities, the balance between formal board/committee meetings and the informal network of discussion is quite different. The relevant department, fire headquarters, PTE offices and so on, are likely to be a considerable distance away from the town hall base of most councillors, making informal discussion with officers difficult. The joint board will usually be serviced on a lead authority basis by one of the district councils concerned, which is fine for councillors from that district, but much less accessible to other joint board members. Unless there has been established a source of information about joint board activities within a joint board member's own authority – for example, the City of Manchester's Police Monitoring Unit (and such units are extremely rare) – then there is unlikely to be an alternative source of briefings available about joint board matters. Informal contact amongst joint board members between formal meetings is likely, if it happens to all, to be confined to the other two or three members from the councillor's own authority. In comparison with a service which is the exclusive responsibility of the district council, joint board matters rarely enjoy the benefit of an informal network, which is such a significant element of intra-authority councillor activity. Thus, most joint board members will inevitably approach formal meetings relatively 'cold'. As John Stewart has aptly pointed out,[19]

> past experience would suggest that the members of a joint board become isolated from the authority nominating them once they pass through the doors of the joint board. Often they do not report back to the local authority, and if they did, who would there be to advise the council on policy on that joint board, whose expertise is comparable with the officers of the joint board?

There are exceptions to this generalisation: the joint board chair, vice-chair and sometimes other joint board members (for example, sub-committee chairs) are often drawn into a 'leadership elite'. It is they who become the main conduit between officer briefings and advice and the decision-making process. It is they (and particularly the chair) who will have regular meetings with lead authority officers and joint board chief officers, and who will often become part of a wider political community relating to that service, including local authority association meetings, conferences, special visits, and so on. This 'special treatment', inevitable in the circumstances, puts the chair and vice-chair at a considerable advantage vis-à-vis their joint board colleagues in relation to detailed knowledge of the issues concerned. As Leach, Davis et al. point out,[20] 'In these circumstances

more weight is bound to be attached to the role of the joint board chairs. ...
The officers will know that if they can convince the chair and vice-chair of
the rights of a particular course of action, it is highly likely to be accepted by
the joint board itself'. It is true that joint board agendas will be discussed
prior to formal meetings by the various party groups represented on the joint
board but, in meetings of the majority party group (assuming there is one), it
is highly unlikely that the advice of the chair and vice-chair will be
challenged. Apart from points of principle (for example, in relation to the use
of plastic bullets) on what basis could the joint board back-bencher do so?

The result, in almost all examples of joint boards studied in our research,
is that the chair of the joint board is in an extremely powerful position and
is much less susceptible to challenge than the chair of a local authority
service committee, for all the reasons outlined above. In this sense
'participative democracy' amongst members of the same political party is
diminished.

INTER-SERVICE CO-ORDINATION AND CHOICE

The creation of joint boards and executive joint committees in the
metropolitan counties is part of a more general process of fragmentation.
Other dimensions of the fragmentation process – for example, CCT,
externalisation, the loss of functions to external non-elected bodies – have
been given greater attention, but the joint boards and executive joint
committees have also contributed to the fragmentation process. It is widely
recognised that (despite the potential strength of departmentalism) it is more
difficult to co-ordinate or integrate the activities of separate organisations
than it is the activities of separate divisions within an organisation.

The problem of joint board-related fragmentation is perhaps best
illustrated in relation to strategic land-use transportation planning. Prior to
1986 responsibility for the planning, highways, public transport and land-
use strategy rested with a single authority in the metropolitan areas. After
1986 responsibilities were divided between a county-wide passenger
transport joint board on the one hand and a number of individual districts on
the other. Although attempts to sustain an integrated view of these problems
were made in relation to the unitary development plan, strategic guidance
documents submitted jointly by districts in the metropolitan counties, which
reflected the setting up of working parties comprising the joint board
officers as well as district planners and engineers, such informal networks
often did not survive the strategic guidance exercise.[21] Leach concludes,[22]

> There is still a very real doubt as to whether the informal networks
> linking land-use planners, highways planners and passenger transport

planners are strong enough to sustain the initial commitment which has been made to the principles of strategic land-use transportation planning in the strategic guidance statements.

The challenge for local authorities to integrate the work of an increasingly diverse set of relevant organisations now goes much wider than the range of functions and responsibilities distributed amongst joint boards and joint committees. The fact that such integration has proved difficult for functions where local councillors dominate the decision-making bodies concerned only underlines the size of the task when such bodies are not councillor-dominated. An increasingly widespread acceptance by local authorities of the principle of partnership has sometimes overlooked the difficulties of the inter-agency co-ordination which is implied.

JOINT BODIES AND THE LOCAL GOVERNMENT REVIEW

The issue of the accountability of joint bodies has become topical again recently in connection with local government reorganisation. In Scotland, Wales, and parts of England, new unitary local authorities are to be established. There are different implications for the range of joint bodies likely to be required. The important distinctions are as follows:

(i)   Situations in which a whole county or region has been split up into unitary authorities.
(ii) Situations, in England, in which two or more unitary authorities have been designated within an otherwise unchanged county area.
(iii) Situations, in England, in which there is a single unitary authority established in an otherwise unchanged county.

In the first category, the situation will be similar to that which pertains in the English metropolitan conurbations (particularly in Strathclyde, Lothian, Avon, Cleveland and Humberside). Joint fire authorities will be established. There is a strong case for executive joint committees to cover strategic land-use transportation planning and waste disposal.[23] (The passenger transport authorities of the metropolitan counties will not be replicated elsewhere – other than Strathclyde – because their creation in the Mets reflected the already existing PTA/PTE structure in relation to passenger transport, which was exclusive to these areas.) Because these areas have a single primary large city-focus the case for additional joint arrangements to deal with issues such as economic development and environmental regeneration is correspondingly stronger. In each area, there will be at least four authorities involved in the joint arrangements, which will mean that no one authority can hope to dominate them.

In the second category – two or more unitary 'islands' in an otherwise unchanged county – joint fire authorities are again to be imposed. The case for an executive joint body in relation to strategic land-use issues varies with the social geography of the county area. It is stronger, for example, in Leicestershire than it is in Devon. However, as the Local Government Commission has failed to differentiate between such situations it can only be assumed that, if voluntary joint action is perceived as ineffective, the government will impose joint arrangements with executive power. In this category, there will often be considerable discrepancies between the representative weight of the participants, particularly on the joint boards. Thus in Hampshire (over one million population) the county council will have far more bargaining muscle in such bodies than Southampton (220,000) or Portsmouth (190,000), or both districts combined. Thus there are important differences in the inter-authority balance in this category, as compared with the county-wide unitary solution. Much greater, however, is the inter-authority imbalance in the many counties where only one unitary authority is to be established. For example, in North Yorkshire and Wiltshire, York and Thamesdown, respectively, will be very much the minor 'partner' compared with the much more populous counties in which they are located.

In one sense these differences in inter-authority influence on joint bodies can be regarded as of only limited relevance. After all, if the new joint boards behave like their metropolitan counterparts, then York's Labour representatives will simply become part of the joint board Labour group – and similarly for the Conservatives and Liberal Democrats. But, if this is the outcome, it will only serve to underline the inoperability of delegate democracy based on the participating authorities, and the 'accountability vacuum' which is associated with current practice on metropolitan joint boards.

CONCLUSIONS

Joint boards and executive joint committees operate in an intermediate position between the direct accountability of local authorities and the opaque accountability processes of appointed bodies. There is a greater level of public debate about the agendas of the former, supported by the comprehensive 'access to information' requirements of local government. It is possible, though not common, to find statements of political intent in local election party manifestos. Debate about joint board issues does take place from time to time within district and London borough councils, although rarely on a systematic basis. All these features of joint bodies can be argued to offer a good deal more in the way of accountability (using the term in a general sense) than is available in the operation of appointed bodies.

However, as has been demonstrated earlier, there are also a number of important differences between local authorities and joint bodies which invariably operate to the disadvantage of the latter. Direct accountability based on representative democracy is clearly impossible in joint bodies because they are not directly elected. With the demise of the Metropolitan Labour Parties, there is now no mechanism through which political choices in relation to the activities of joint bodies can be put before local electorates. Indirect accountability in which the members of joint boards are mandated by the constituent councils is possible in theory, but little practised in reality, and in the case of minority party representatives on joint boards it is quite unrealistic to expect the acceptance of majority party mandates. Given the arm's length nature of joint bodies, considerable potential power accrues to the chair and councillors are in a much weaker position, legally and in practice, to challenge the professional advice of the officers advising them. Co-ordination between joint board services and other related services is more difficult than if the services were all the responsibility of the same authority. Similarly, the scope for political choice in the resource allocation between joint board services and other services is reduced in scope. The main potential benefits of what are, in effect, single-purpose agencies are those which flow from a single-minded focus on the service in question.

The government recognises that executive joint arrangements dilute the principle of unitary local government. The Local Government Commission recognises it also. Yet both the government and the commission have continued to refer to the existence of unitary local authorities in Greater London and the metropolitan counties. It is clear from the post-abolition experience of these areas that to argue that a unitary system is in existence there is an illusion. Metropolitan districts and London boroughs recognise this reality and we have yet to hear a convincing refutation of one of the key conclusions of our *After Abolition* report,[24] 'the most appropriate way to regard the 1986 reorganisation in the metropolitan counties (and in Greater London, where the situation is similar) is a transition from *one form of metropolitan government* – a two-tier system with a *directly*-elected upper tier – to *another* – a two-tier system with an *indirectly*-elected upper tier'. As argued above, the new so-called unitary authorities in England, Wales and Scotland fall into the same category, the unitary myth rather than the unitary reality, because of the range of executive joint arrangements required for the effective exercise of local functions.

Given the increasing fragmentation of local service provision responsibilities, it could be argued that a handful of joint boards and executive joint committees make little difference to the external dependencies facing individual local authorities. If networking, partnership, negotiation and the management of influence are the new realities, then joint boards are in principle more amenable to such processes than training and enterprise councils, health authorities, chambers of commerce and further education colleges, because at least they consist wholly or mainly of local councillors. What has been a problem is the way the nature and significance of joint bodies have been used and abused in the debate about local government reorganisation in Scotland and Wales and the shire areas of England.

NOTES

1 . J. Stewart, 'The Conditions of Joint Action', *London Journal,* Vol.10, No.1 (1985), pp.59–65.
2. Department of the Environment, *Revised Policy Guidance to the Local Government Commission for England* (Nov. 1993), para.15.
3. The different forms of organisational joint arrangements (for example, lead authority, jointly financed specialist unit, and so on) are not discussed here.
4. See C.A. Cross, *Principles of Local Government Law* (Sweet and Maxwell, 1982), p.78.
5. Ibid., p.79.
6. See N. Flynn and S. Leach, *Joint Boards and Joint Committees: An Evaluation* (INLOGOV: The University of Birmingham, 1984), p.27; and F.J.C. Cheetham, 'Local Government Reorganisation and the Museum Service', *The Museums Journal,* Vol.74, No.1 (1974).
7. See N. Flynn and S. Leach, op. cit., pp.30–31.
8. Department of the Environment, op. cit., para.14.
9. See S. Leach, H. Davis, C. Game and C. Skelcher, *After Abolition: The Operation of the Post 1986 Metropolitan Government System in England* (INLOGOV: The University of Birmingham, 1992), pp.294–5.
10. It has been calculated that 75 per cent of the net current expenditure of the metropolitan county councils was transferred in 1986 to joint bodies (see S. Leach *et al.,* op. cit., p.3).
11 . Ibid., p.132.
12. Ibid., p.138.
13. J. Gyford, S. Leach and C. Game, *The Changing Politics of Local Government* (Unwin Hyman, 1989), p.346.
14. Speech by Patrick Jenkin, *Hansard,* 3 Dec. 1984, cols.32–5.
15. S. Leach *et al.,* op. cit., p.138.
16. See S. Leach, 'Metropolitan Labour Parties: Scope Sanctions and Strategy, *Local Government Studies,* Vol.14, No.4 (1988), pp.1–8.
17. S. Leach, 'Accountability in the Post-Abolition Metropolitan Government System', *Local Government Studies,* Vol.16, No.3 (1990), p.29.
18. Ibid., pp.30–31.
19. J. Stewart, op. cit., p.62.
20. S. Leach *et al.,* op. cit., p.110.
21. S. Leach, 'Strategic Land-Use Transportation Planning: The Implications of Post-Abolition Experience', *Strategic Government,* Vol.1, No.1 (1992), pp.27–8.
22. Ibid., p.29.
23. As acknowledged by the Local Government Commission itself. See Local Government Commission for England, *Renewing Local Government in the English Shires: A Progress Report* (1993), pp.23–7.
24. S. Leach *et al.,* op. cit., pp.3–4.

Lessons from Local Government in Northern Ireland

MICHAEL CONNOLLY

INTRODUCTION

A number of commentators have argued that in Britain there has been a return to a new magistracy, in which elected local government has been diminished at the expense of appointed bodies.[1] This article focuses on the experience in Northern Ireland. This is interesting for a number of reasons, especially because the logical outcome of the model of reduced local government (short of actually abolishing local government) exists in Northern Ireland, where the 1972 Local Government (NI) Act greatly diminished the role and status of local government. This occurred partly because of the geographical and economic structure of Northern Ireland, but mostly because of political violence and divided society. The proximate cause of this violence arose from what members of the minority nationalist community believed was an elected dictatorship, in which there was a combination of demographics (the unionist community having approximately 60 per cent of the population) and questionable political actions on such matters as local government ward boundaries. As a result, the importance of local political structures were diminished. Hence an important argument, presented by almost all members of the nationalist community, as well as a significant number of unionists, for the growth in appointed books and the decline of elected bodies was – and continues to be – that the minority community stood a better chance of being represented in the former. This might be thought to be different from the situation in Britain, where the suspicion predominates that the rise in quangos was to enable the government to place its own supporters in situations of influence and reward.

There is a second reason for examining the Northern Ireland case, in that it represents a situation familiar and yet remarkably different from the rest of the UK. The familiarity arises because Northern Ireland is a part of the UK and for most of the past 70 years was governed according to British constitutional principles (or at least a form of them). The difference arises

Michael Connolly, University of Glamorgan

because the politics of Northern Ireland are more violent and occupy a different set of concerns – at least in intensity – compared with other parts of the Kingdom. Students of public administration (if there are still students of such an outmoded discipline) have a social prism through which the principles of the British constitution might be explored.[2] The theme of this article is the impact on representation and accountability as a result of the changes to local governance in Northern Ireland. Initially we shall describe the system of local government in more detail.

LOCAL GOVERNMENT IN NORTHERN IRELAND

The present local government system dates from 1973, when the Local Government (NI) Act (1972) abolished the local government system then in operation, a system which had largely remained unchanged since it was set up under the Local Government (Ireland) Act of 1898. The 1972 Act provided for the constitution of district councils to administer the 26 local government districts and for the regulation of such councils and certain of their functions.

Criticisms of local government had been a central part of the critique of the Unionist government by the civil rights movement and other like-minded political groups. For example, the cry of 'One Man, One Vote', which was such an emotive rallying call during many of the early civil rights marches, was directed at the local government franchise. This is not the place to repeat the various debates about the validity, or otherwise, of the various criticisms.[3] But it is perhaps worth stating that it was generally accepted that the behaviour of some, at least, of the councils in relation to even-handedness between the two communities left something to be desired. This contributed to the belief, still held by many, particularly nationalists, that councillors were not to be trusted and that the best way of minimising any damage they might cause was to limit their powers. Given our concerns in this article, this point needs to be emphasised, as it contributes to the acceptance of the many quangos (albeit with reservations) by individuals and political parties who normally would be critical of the idea.

In October 1969 it was decided 'reluctantly that the local authorities are not geared – and cannot be geared – to handle (housing) and that the best hope of success lies in the creation of a single-purpose, efficient and streamlined central housing authority'.[4] This authority was to take over responsibility for the building, management and allocation of all public housing from the local authorities, the Northern Ireland Housing Trust and the three Development Commissions.[5]

The creation of the Northern Ireland Housing Executive (NIHE), at one and the same time, removed one of the most controversial functions from the local authorities and necessitated a radical investigation into local government. As a result, a review body on local government was set up by the Stormont government in December 1969, under the chairmanship of Patrick Macrory to 'advise on the most efficient distribution under the Parliament and Government of Northern Ireland – whether under local government or otherwise – of the functions (of local government)'.

MACRORY REPORT

The review body reported in June 1970. Central to its analysis was the broad classification of regional and district services used by the Wheatley Report on local government in Scotland. The case for health and personal social services as an integrated regional service had been made in a green paper in July 1969. Macrory judged a number of other services as regional and these became the responsibility of area boards (for example, education and library services), or government departments (for example, the DOE(NI)) acquired direct responsibility for planning, road, water and sewerage), or centralised *ad hoc* boards (for example, the fire service) (see Table 1 for further details).

TABLE 1
PRINCIPAL DELIVERY AGENTS FOR LOCAL SERVICES

	Government Departments	Centralised Boards	Area Boards	Local Government
Health			*	
Personal Social Services			*	
Education			*	
Housing		*		
Town & Country Planning	*			
Roads	*			
Water & Sewerage	*			
Recreation				*
Economic Development	*			
Fire Services		*		

Source: Adapted from Birrell and Murie, *Policy and Government in Northern Ireland* (Gill and MacMillan, 1980), p.174.

What then was to be the structure and functions of local government? The report argued for a reduction in the number of local authorities from 72 to 26 district councils.[6] These were to have four functions, as follows.

(1) *Ceremonial functions* which refer to the dignities and ceremonial traditionally attached to local government.
(2) *Executive functions,* that is, the provision of services.
(3) *Representative functions,* by which Macrory meant that local councils should be represented upon relevant bodies, such as area boards, so as 'to express views on the provision and operations of ... public services in their area'.[7]
(4) *Consultative functions* involving the consultation of the district councils on matters of general national interest as well as those which are the responsibility of central government but affect their area, for example, planning applications, housing and roads.

EXECUTIVE FUNCTIONS

Given the range of services deemed to be regional, little in the way of executive functions was left to the local authorities. Local authorities are responsible for services such as street cleaning, refuse collection and disposal, burial grounds and crematoria, public baths, recreation facilities and tourist amenities. In addition, councils have regulatory powers over a number of services including licensing of cinemas, dance-halls and street-trading, building regulations and health inspection. Local authorities have a limited number of other powers, including, for example, the ability to spend certain monies for the general welfare of the people within the area. There have been some minor adjustments made to these services since 1972, most lately in the 1992 Order, which gave to local authorities powers to spend monies for economic development, subject to certain constraints.[8]

REPRESENTATIVE AND CONSULTATIVE FUNCTIONS

These functions were seen as important and as ensuring that local interests would be represented in decision making in areas such as education, personal social services, planning and housing. In short, it was recognised that local government had a place within the governance of local areas. There have, however, been some shifts in their formal involvement.

Education and related services, including the library services, are managed through five education and library boards, 40 per cent of the members of which are local councillors. The recent reforms in education, which in Northern Ireland have been enacted in the Education Reform (NI) Order 1989,[9] and include the introduction of LMS, have raised questions about the continued role and structure of the boards. A 1993 consultative paper[10] outlined a number of alternative models of the possible future structure of education administration, some of which would reduce further the role of local government in education. For example, one model argued for the rationalisation of (that is, reduction in) the number of boards. The paper indicated that a reduction in the size of board membership would be desirable. The problem, which the paper raises, is how to accommodate the interests of local authorities in such a model. One suggestion made, for example, is to reduce the number of education boards and to create education councils analogous to health and personal social services councils which are consumer bodies with rights of consultation but not of executive decision making. The minister responsible for education in a speech in April 1995 proposed reducing the number of boards to four, amalgamating the areas associated with the South Eastern Board with the Belfast and Southern Boards, as well as a number of other proposals for regionalising services. More recently (September 1995) he indicated that he did not wish to go ahead with the amalgamation, partly because locally elected representatives were not convinced of the proposal. Instead he has invited the political parties to examine with him the economic and educational options available to him. It is clear from his statement that he favours the amalgamation proposal and it will be interesting to see the outcome of his discussions with the parties.

Since 1972 *health and personal social services* have been administered differently in Northern Ireland compared with the rest of the UK. Five integrated health and social service boards, responsible to the DHSS(NI), were created at that time. Initially the percentage of councillor membership was 30 per cent – all appointed by the minister following nomination by their respective councils. The remainder of board members comprised individuals drawn from professional bodies, interested groups and other local people, appointed by the relevant minister.

As a result of the *Working for Patients* reforms, the composition of the boards was radically altered in line with similar initiatives in the rest of the UK. Boards are now much smaller, and consist of a chair, up to five executive members and five non-executive members, the latter being appointed by the mnister. No longer are councillors automatically members and indeed the bulk of first appointments were not councillors.[11]

Councillors are involved in the Health and Personal Social Services Councils, mentioned above. Further, a number of councils have set up health committees, whose purpose is to seek to influence the HPSS boards and the DHSS(NI), particularly over such issues as hospital closures. In general, local government has little influence on health and personal social services matters, though particular councillors may be particularly influential because of personality, knowledge or political influence.

Local government is involved formally in *housing* in a number of ways. At a policy level, each of the 26 councils is represented on the Housing Council, which gives policy advice to the NIHE and DOE(NI) and elects three out of the ten members of the board of the executive. In addition, the chief executive of the NIHE, with appropriate colleagues, appears at district council meetings to explain housing policy as it affects that district. These meetings are supposedly concerned with the new building programme, but other issues ranging from general policy matters to the quality of the maintenance programme in the district can arise.

With respect to *planning* and *roads,* local authorities are consulted by the relevant division within the DOE(NI) over matters that affect their district. Thus planning officers bring applications within the district area to councils with their recommendations. In the case of disagreements, site visits are arranged and a process of debate occurs, though at the end of the day councillors are *consulted* and it is clear that responsibility for decision-making lies with the DOE(NI) planners.

In the case of roads, the council is visited by the regional roads manger who discusses such matters as the roads maintenance programme with the council. Again he/she listens to the views of councillors, who have some influence on priorities and developments, but the final decision lies with the DOE(NI).

ELECTORAL REFORM

This, then, is a basic description of the local government system in Northern Ireland. To complete this and to make a further important point of comparison with the British local government system we need to comment on the electoral system. 'One Man, One Vote' had been an important cry of the civil rights campaign in the late 1960s in Northern Ireland with, as already stated, the electoral practices of local authorities regarded with suspicion. An additional issue was that political parties which sought to cross the sectarian division did not achieve much in the way of electoral success. One proposal to escape both problems was to reform the electoral system. Hence the single transferable vote (STV) system of proportional representation was introduced under the Electoral Law (Northern Ireland) Order 1972, initially as an experiment. In 1977, the Northern Ireland (Local Elections) Order provided for STV to be used for all future district council elections. The reform was introduced to considerable Unionist opposition, which is less vocal but still persistent.[12]

Despite the lack of powers, turnout for local government elections in Northern Ireland remains relatively high. In May 1989 the turnout was 57.4 per cent, with significantly higher figures in the western councils and lower figures nearer Belfast. Further, as in the rest of the UK, political parties are dominant, with few independent councillors or candidates (though one council – Moyle – has a majority of independent councillors).

EXPERIENCE OF THE NORTHERN IRELAND SYSTEM

This, then, was the system introduced in 1972 and which has broadly remained in place since that date. The system has meant a greatly reduced role for direct provision of locally elected services, but an explicit, limited and changing role for local authorities in the governance of Northern Ireland.

The system has operated against the backcloth of continuing political violence and the attempt to find an agreed solution. This has meant that there has been a reluctance to tamper with the current arrangements, however flawed. Any radical reform, for example the restoration of powers to local authorities (something argued by many unionists), was never seriously on the agenda as such a proposition either had to come out of a political solution or would herald the abandonment of any attempt to find a solution. For example, nationalists would regard a radical shift of power to local authorities as a unionist solution and hence would reject it.

EQUITY, EFFICIENCY AND EFFECTIVENESS OF SERVICES

There is little doubt that public services are managed much more impartially than before. There are a number of watchdog organisations, including the Ombudsman and the Fair Employment Commission (FEC) and its previous incarnation, the Fair Employment Agency (FEA), and their reports clearly suggest that sectarianism in administration appears not to be a major issue.

With respect to employment, the FEA/FEC has conducted investigations into the employment practices of a variety of public sector organisations including the Housing Executive, area boards and a number of local authorities. The FEA report in 1985 on the Housing Executive concluded that the organisation was providing equal opportunities for both sections of the community. Both sets of area boards, while not having an entirely clean bill of health, in general have acceptable records.

The major area of continuing difficulty with respect to employment practices are the local authorities, a number of whom resent the activities of the FEC/FEA. Some unionist-controlled councils, for example, refused the FEA's invitation to sign a declaration of commitment to the principle of equality of opportunity. In 1992, five councils were found guilty of unlawful discrimination. In March 1994, five Catholics were awarded substantial damages against Belfast Council as a result of FEC rulings.

A continuing major concern remains the low representation of Catholics among senior staff across the public sector, and more particularly across local authorities. According to the Fair Employment Commission,[13] 22 per cent of the senior staff in local government are Catholics, a figure which is

2.3 per cent lower than in the public sector as a whole. But across local councils recruitment procedures are now much more bureaucratised and officials, at least, are sensitive to the implications of the FEC and recommendations emanating from it.

One interesting area the FEC has not explored is the representation on the various QUANGOs. Given the significance of this issue in Northern Ireland this might be thought to be an important omission. The contrast between securing appointment to a board and obtaining employment with the same board is stark. The latter is increasingly the subject of scrutiny and procedures while the former is a closed book.

The question of equity of service delivery between the two communities is a more controversial issue, with representatives of both communities still prepared to charge that their community is losing out in the allocation of resources. Hard evidence is difficult to come by.[14] In general, however, it is widely accepted that the delivery of public services is much more even-handed between the communities now, compared with the pre-local government reform position. It has, however, to be stressed that a number of commentators and unionist politicians resist the suggestion that there were any major inequities in the old system.[15] On the other hand, Cormack et al.[16] in their research indicated that the Catholic community received a smaller proportion of resources in education than might have been expected. It is unlikely that such research would have appeared, or had the impact it has had, under the Stormont regime.

Livingston and Morison[17] have argued that the government has adopted a more explicit concern with the impact of policies on the two communities. The central Community Relations Unit of the Northern Ireland Office has developed policy appraisal and fair treatment (PAFT) guidelines. These require government organisations to consider whether their policies may have a differential impact on a particular group and, if this is found to be the case, such bodies must consider whether the policy must be modified or abandoned. This indicates that the government is taking an active role in managing the relations between the two communities, as well as between the communities and the state.

The role of the police remains the most contentious aspect of these relationships and their governance has come under intense debate, fuelled by the cease-fire. The Royal Ulster Constabulary (RUC) is managed by a tripartite arrangement, involving the NIO, the chief constable and the police authority for Northern Ireland.[18] The authority, which was created as an attempt to introduce greater accountability, has always confronted a series of problems which have inhibited its ability to do its job. The IRA murdered some of its members, necessitating membership to become anonymous. The trade unions and the SDLP refused to nominate members, again reducing its ability to function as a vehicle for police accountability to the general public. Finally, the violence meant that criticisms of the police were seen as unusually political and likely to be portrayed as helping the paramilitaries. The cease-fire, together with the appointment of a more open and politically aware chair, has meant that the debate about the role of the police and the mechanisms of accountability has become more open and will undoubtedly form part of the final political settlement.

It is probably true that in a region as small as Northern Ireland there were efficiency gains from reducing the number of organisations involved in service delivery. Concern remains that some local authorities are too small to be viable and, as already indicated, the Minister for Education has argued that five education and library boards is at least one too many. Further he has sought to regionalise a number of services on the grounds of efficiency.

There is little evidence on the performance of councils. The sort of performance tables which are beloved of the Audit Commission are much rarer birds in Northern Ireland. The NIAO,[19] for example, complained that there has not been sufficient comparative analysis of the provision and cost of local authorities' services. Studies of leisure services[20] suggest that a number of Northern Ireland local authorities have been very generous in their provision of facilities. Belfast, for example, has been described as the United Kingdom's most lavish local authority,[21] with 14 leisure centres as compared with the five or six which should be its entitlement calculated on the Sports Council's planning standards. Part of this reflects the need to provide divided communities with leisure facilities, though this in turn has provoked political controversy. It might be argued that it is evidence of the greater sensitivity of local councils to the needs of local communities and contrasts with, for example, the planning service, where it is alleged that the sensitivities of rural communities are not always taken fully into account in decision making.

MACRORY GAP

Whatever the gains in efficiency, equity and effectiveness of services, these have been achieved at the expense of democratic accountability. As already indicated, government by appointment has been introduced with greater force and breadth in Northern Ireland than elsewhere in the UK. Indeed, given the removal of councillors from HPSS boards and possibly education and library boards, there will be an even smaller role for elected representatives in the governance of public services in future.

To be fair, the Macrory Report was predicated upon the continuing existence of Stormont, the regional parliament. However, the violence that had played such a prominent feature in the reforms of local government continued to increase through the early 1970s. Eventually the British government prorogued Stormont and took direct responsibility for the government of Northern Ireland through the creation of the post of Secretary of State for Northern Ireland. This meant that the regional services were no longer accountable to Northern Ireland politicians. The problem is further compounded in that normal parliamentary procedures are not applied to a wide range of Northern Ireland affairs, including much legislation.[22]

Influenced no doubt by wider charges about lack of accountability, central government has been sensitive to the accusation that local government has too few services and too limited a role. Fears about the political consequences of returning major services to local government have ensured that no radical structural changes have taken – or are likely to take – place. But there have been efforts to increase local government's responsibilities and activities. For example, during the last Labour government, there was a substantial increase, encouraged by central government, in local government interest in leisure, particularly in the building of leisure facilities, with the consequences described earlier.

Councils themselves have sought to increase their role. For example, in the early 1980s they became interested in local economic development.[23] This involved the use of their powers under sections 107 and 115 of the 1972 Act. Under the former, local councils may contribute 'towards the expenses of any voluntary body which carried on activities … for the purposes of furthering the development of trade and industry or commerce'. Section 115 allows councils to spend up to 0.5p in the pound rate for any purpose which is in the interest of the people in its district.

Central government has had some reservations about local authorities' activities in this area, fearing that they will attempt initiatives for which they are ill-equipped. Nevertheless, they recognised that many local authorities were interested in making a contribution to the development of their local area. Hence the 1992 Local Government (Miscellaneous Provisions) (Northern Ireland) Order gave local authorities power to spend money to promote the economic development of their areas, provided that they have obtained prior approval from the DOE(NI). There was no attempt to define economic development and the department has indicated that it will be sympathetic to any proposals, provided that they do not conflict with the work of bodies such as the Industrial Development Board and the Local Enterprise Development Unit.

Some local authorities have sought to use such powers as they have, together with networking across a range of national and international agencies, to contribute to local economic and social development. Armagh has, for example, sought to develop an economic development strategy around tourism by engaging a range of agencies to contribute funds.

These efforts have had political implications, in that councils seeking to network believe that they are more likely to succeed if they are seen as representing cross-community interests. This has contributed to the increase in councils willing to 'share power'. In the Northern Ireland context this means that senior council posts such as council chair are shared between members of political parties across the political divide. Such efforts usually involve members of the Social Democratic and Labour Party (moderate nationalist), the Alliance Party (a moderate unionist party which draws votes across both communities) and the Official Unionists. In general, the Democratic Unionist Party, led by Ian Paisley, is not happy with power-sharing arrangements involving non-Unionists. The role of Sinn Fein is an interesting one. Despite the cease-fire, unionists continue to dislike their presence on councils and would seek to exclude them from any power-sharing arrangement. On the other hand, Omagh, where Sinn Fein is the largest party, has had a long-standing power-sharing arrangement.

LOCAL GOVERNMENT AND THE MAKING OF POLICY

Two interrelated trends are detectable about the policy process in Northern Ireland, namely the growing convergence of policy between Northern Ireland and the rest of the UK, and the dominance of Northern Ireland departments and the Northern Ireland civil service in policy making within Northern Ireland. In part this is due to the creation of the office of Secretary of State, which helped to integrate public policy in Northern Ireland with the rest of the UK. The Secretary of State is a British politician, belonging to a national (as opposed to Northern Ireland-based) political party. While there has always been a sense that Northern Ireland is different, increasingly ministers are asking in what way, and what impact should this have on policy developments? As this UK dimension increases, the influence of the Secretary of State and his colleagues will strengthen as they are the essential channel of communication between Northern Ireland and the rest of the UK. In turn, this will enhance the influence of the civil servants, given their close relationship with ministers.

This trend has also been assisted by the reforms of government structure described earlier. These have greatly strengthened the role of government departments. For example, while relationships between boards and their respective departments are on occasion fraught, there can be little doubt that the latter is the dominant partner. Boards receive virtually all their money from their respective department. They are accountable to the department for their expenditure and operate within departmental policy guidelines. In addition, the health and personal social service boards are formally defined as agents of the Department of Health and Social Services.

Within this broad context it would appear that whatever the formal role of councillors on the various agencies their influence is minimal. This is something that many councils, especially those dominated by Official Unionists and Democratic Unionists, resent. Councillors feel frustrated that they can only voice complaints and act as a lobby, instead of controlling services directly. Their role is essentially one of being a vehicle for the concerns of constituents who, despite the limited formal powers of councillors, still regard them as important channels of influence. Officers from the various agencies who attend council meetings to explain *policy* matters feel irritated that the discussion quickly turns to the concerns of individual constituents of councillors. Yet for councillors there is little political benefit to be derived from general policy concerns. Their interests are to be re-elected, and being seen to be active on behalf of their constituents is important in this respect. In a number of councils this will take the form of the creation of sub-committees on subjects such as health. Such committees seek to influence board developments, examining policy pronouncements with a particular eye as to their local implications.

The attitude of officials to councillors in part reflects the above. Many officials tend to denigrate politicians and accuse them of irresponsibility. In part this stems from a belief that councillors can only make trouble for officials. The result is a built-in tension within the system, with councillors encouraged to act 'irresponsibly', to simply attack public agencies, government departments and officials. Councillors feel no ownership of decisions that emerge from existing institutions. It is not unknown for councillors to participate in a decision of a public agency through membership of a board and then to attack it in the council or some other public platform.

The electoral system also has a role in encouraging this behaviour among councillors. The STV system means that a councillor seeking election is in competition with her/his colleagues as well as nominal opponents. Indeed, because of the sectarian divide, as a result of which there is relatively little cross-community voting, there is a sense in which electoral competition is focused within each community. Unionists are in competition with each other rather than Nationalists, and the same is true in respect of Nationalists. One – perhaps the key – strategy in this situation is to ensure that you are, and/or are seen to be, representing your constituents' interests.

One further aspect of this is the quality of councillors. There is a widespread belief that the intellectual abilities of councillors are limited, that fewer middle-class and university-educated people are becoming councillors. In fact, there is limited empirical evidence on this matter, though such evidence as exists throws doubts on this view. Birrell,[24] in a comparison of those councillors elected in the 1973 and 1979 elections, found that councillors in the new system appear to be better educated than those in the old system, though there were considerable differences between parties, with the Alliance and SDLP parties having the highest percentages of university-educated people. Further, new councillors were younger and better educated than their predecessors (and the population as a whole). In addition, women are still underrepresented on councils.[25] The widespread view is that 20 years of political violence and the relative impotence of local authorities have taken their toll, and fewer good people are interested in coming forward for election to councils. However, more recent data on the social characteristics of councillors would help to discern trends.

CONCLUSION

As a result of various reforms, governmental structures with Northern Ireland have been altered radically since the early 1970s. There are clear and obvious differences between the structure in Northern Ireland and the rest of the United Kingdom. The balancing of concerns about efficiency and effectiveness, as well as impartiality, with those of democratic accountability is a perennial difficulty in public administration. In Northern Ireland local authorities have executive responsibility for fewer services and there is a much greater attempt to take services 'out of politics' through the use of non-elected public bodies. Public officials – whether they are civil servants, local government officers or professionals – have grown in importance at the expense of politicians, particularly local politicians. Northern Ireland has not been unique in attempting to manage public services through endeavouring to depoliticise them, but this approach to policy management has perhaps gone further in Northern Ireland than elsewhere in the UK. Partly this reflects a widespread tendency to distrust politicians, and a view that services are best left to professionals and administrators, but in the main it is an attempt to escape some of the baser features of sectarian politics. But the price in Northern Ireland has been a distrust of the system from a substantial part of the population and considerable tension between politicians and administrators.

However, perhaps the main lesson to be drawn from the Northern Ireland system is that politics is an inevitable part of local government. Even when local government is denuded of other roles, councillors seek to play a political role. Indeed the evidence from Northern Ireland suggests that the political role expands when other roles are eliminated. Further, when the importance of local government is diminished, this has important consequences for the quality and attitude of councillors and their relationship with officials. Even in such circumstances, many local councillors seek to act in the best interests of their area and, as a result, local councils in Northern Ireland engage in a wide range of networking activities. The political imperative of doing something and being seen to be doing something about community development, particularly in the economic sphere has to be satisfied.

NOTES

1. M. Clarke and J. Stewart, 'From Traditional Management to the New Management in British Local Government,' *Policy Studies Journal,* 21, 1 (1993) pp.82–93; J. Stewart, A. Greer and P. Hoggett, 'The Quango State: An Alternative Approach, Commission on Local Democracy', Research Report No.10, Feb. 1995.
2. This is the interesting perspective adopted by. J. Morison and S. Livingstone in their book, *Reshaping Public Power: Northern Ireland and the British Constitutional Crisis* (Sweet and Maxwell, 1995).
3. *Disturbances In Northern Ireland: Report Of The Commission Appointed By The Governor Of Northern Ireland* (Cameron Report) Cmd. 532 (Belfast: HMSO, 1969); J. Whyte, 'How Much Discrimination was there under the Unionist Regime, 1921–69?', in T. Gallagher and J. O'Connell, *Contemporary Irish Studies* (Manchester University Press, 1983).
4. Text of a Communique, Cmnd.4178 (HMSO, 1969).
5. The Housing Trust was a public agency set up in 1945 to augment the work of the local authorities in housing. The development commissions were created during the 1960s for special projects, for example the Londonderry Commission was created to take over the building of houses in Londonderry (D. Birrell and A. Murie, *Policing and Government in Northern Ireland: Lessons of Devolution* (Gill and Macmillan, 1980)). This illustrates the point that QUANGOs were alive and well in Northern Ireland under the old Stormont regime, though it is certainly true that their numbers have increased in recent years.
6. *Review Body on Local Government in Northern Ireland* (Macrory Report), (HMSO, 1969), para.114.
7. Ibid., para.123, p.43.
8. See M. Connolly, *Lessons from Local Government in Northern Ireland* (Local Government Management Board, 1995) for further details and a discussion of some of the financial implications.
9. See P. McKeown and M. Connolly, 'Education reform in Northern Ireland: Maintaining the Distance?, *Journal of Social Policy,* 21 (1992), pp.211–32; and R. Osborne, R. Cormack and A. Gallagher, *After the Reforms: Education and Policy in Northern Ireland* (Avebury, 1993).
10. Department of Education for Northern Ireland, *Education Administration in Northern Ireland: A Consultative Document* (Department of Education for Northern Ireland, 1993).
11. M. Connolly and M. Russell, 'April 1991 and Beyond: Are Health and Social Services Boards Catching the Tide of Change?' *Public Policy and Administration,* Vol.8, No.2 (1993), pp.42–53.
12. M. Connolly and C. Knox, 'Reflections on The 1985 Local Government Elections in Northern Ireland', *Local Government Studies,* Vol.12, No.2 (1986), pp.15–29.
13. Fair Employment Commission for Northern Ireland, *Third Annual Report 1991–92.*
14. See M. Connolly, 'Public Administration in a Conflict Situation: The Case of Northern Ireland', *Governance,* Vol.6, No.1 (1993), pp.79–98.
15. See Whyte, op. cit., for a good review of the arguments.
16. R.J. Cormack, A.M. Gallagher and R.D. Osborne, *Religious Affiliation and Educational Attainment in Northern Ireland* (Standing Advisory Commission on Human Rights, 1991).
17. S. Livingstone and J. Morison, *An Audit of Democracy in Northern Ireland,* Supplement with *Fortnight,* No. 337 (1994).

18. For a detailed examination of recent debates see M. Connolly, J. Law and I. Topping, 'Policing Structures and Police Accountability in Northern Ireland, *Local Government Studies,* forthcoming.

19. Report by the Comptroller and Auditor General for Northern Ireland, Northern Ireland Audit Office (NIAO), *Economy, Efficiency and Effectiveness: Examinations of Certain Matters* (HMSO, 1991).

20. C. Knox, 'Policy evaluation in Leisure Services – The Northern Ireland Case', *Leisure Studies,* 10 (1991), pp.105–17.

21. Ibid., p.108.

22. See B. Hadfield, 'Direct Rule, Delegated Legislation and Parliament', in H. Hayes and P. O'Higgins (eds.), *Lessons from Northern Ireland* (SLS, 1990); and Connolly, op. cit.

23. M. Connolly and M. Murray, 'Local Authority Economic Development in Northern Ireland', *Local Government Studies,* 12, 5 (1986) pp.51–60.

24. D. Birrell, *Local Government Councillors In Northern Ireland,* CSSP Studies No. 83 (University of Strathclyde, 1981).

25. R. Wilford, R. Miller, Y. Bell and F. Donoghue, 'In Their Own Voices: Women Councillors in Northern Ireland', *Public Administration,* 71, 3 (1993), pp.341–55.

'Working the Network': Local Authority Strategies in the Reticulated Local State

DAVID PRIOR

The focus of this article is on the role of local authorities in the new networks of local governance. I will explore three aspects of this emerging role. First, I will examine briefly the context of political, economic and social change in which the emergence of local governance networks can be situated. Second, I will discuss in some detail the actual nature of 'networks', in particular the different forms that inter-agency relationships take within networks. Finally, I will conclude with a very brief consideration of the extent to which working within networks suggests change in the way in which local authorities engage in processes of strategy development and policy making.

THE CONTEXT OF CHANGE

Local governance networks have developed during a period of very considerable change in the systems of values, institutions and practices through which social, economic and political life is organised. Many commentators see this change as signalling a decisive shift from one globally dominant mode of democratic capitalist system to another, albeit not yet clearly defined, mode.[1] In the former, key roles are played by Keynesian economics, 'Fordist' production methods, social norms and institutions which support mass consumption, and the nation state as the pre-eminent form of political expression. The distinguishing characteristics of the latter are taken to include supply-side economic management, flexible and individualised systems of production and consumption, highly differentiated social and cultural norms and institutions, and a declining role for national governments. If there is as yet no clear consensus on the structure and dynamics of the new system, there is a wide measure of agreement that the old system is passing; that we are experiencing an historical period of profound transition on a world scale.

Approaches to understanding the specific experience of local government in this period of major world change – and, even more

David Prior, Birmingham City Council

narrowly, the British local government experience – can be summarised under two main themes.[2] One is concerned with changes in the way local government is organised and managed: the focus is on change in the institutional arrangements for the implementation of public policy at local level. The second theme is concerned with changes in the role of local government within the process of capitalist production and reproduction: the focus is on the relationship between the policy outputs of the local state and the activity of the local economy.

The principal dynamic for change in the organisation and management of local government and local public services is the redefinition of public policy concerns away from a notion of citizenship based in universal rights to a standardised and state-provided range of welfare services, to a citizenship based in the rights of consumers to choose whether and how to meet their welfare needs, with a market of competing providers determining the range, price and quality of services.[3] Tied into this consumerist welfare model, and indeed shaping much of its development, is the application of severe constraints on public service spending, so that the management of public policy is strongly geared towards controlling costs and maximising resource eficiency. The overall effect is the increasing dominance of commercial models of organisation and management throughout the public sector. This does not necessarily imply the straightforward transfer of private sector management practices, rather it signals the emergence of a new and distinctive approach to public sector management based on certain principles and techniques adapted from the business world.[4]

Fundamental to this approach is a system of 'management through contracts' rather than 'control through hierarchy': the consequence of the application of this approach within local government is that 'The old system of direct overseeing of provision is giving way to a more indirect arms-length form of management'.[5] The traditional command structure of public administration is being fragmented into an internal network of trading accounts and client/contractor relations, affecting both the professional-bureaucratic organisation of service functions and the political structures through which those functions are controlled by elected members.[6] Moreover, as service functions become opened up to competition, so the network of contract-based relations extends into the private and voluntary sectors as non-state organisations become providers of public services contracted to the local government client.

Change in the nature of local government's role within the socio-economic system of capitalist democracy is driven by the demands of the increasing global mobility of capital. The global economy, as it moves out of the 'Fordist' era, requires a high degree of local specificity in providing conditions for production and reproduction. National governments lack sufficiently sensitive policy levers to enable them to create such conditions, opening up a space for local economic action which locally based interests can fill. This, it is argued, points to a growing significance of the local state in the development of new forms of relationship between the spheres of economic and political activity.[7]

Local governments have responded by developing an approach to economic policy based on an assessment of their locality's unique socio-economic assets and institutional capacities. This assessment of advantages and opportunities provides the foundation for strategies 'to strengthen existing and potential indigenous resources';[8] local economic development becomes a strategy for *the institutional development of the local economy* rather than a policy aimed at outbidding other localities in a contest to attract footloose national and international investment.[9] It also, inevitably, involves the local authority in a much more developed and interactive set of relationships with the range of non-state agencies in the area in whose control lie many of the existing and potential resources.[10]

Such strategies, however, have implications which stretch beyond the economic policy concerns of local governments. They

> have produced the effect of gradually undermining the traditional sharp distinctions between different policy areas. This is particularly true in the case of labour market and social policy domains, but equally, educational, environmental and cultural policies have become more integrated with ... economic development measures.[11]

Since, in many of these domains, local government has only a limited capacity to act directly, the strategic policy concern of the local authority becomes redefined in an holistic sense as the overall well-being of the locality it governs and the aggregate activities of all the local agencies. It must give attention to the totality of the area's strengths and weaknesses, its resources and its needs, encompassing the private and voluntary sectors as well as other public sector organisations. The policy impact of local government has then to be measured by its success in shaping the 'performance' of the area overall, not just by the outputs of the services it directly controls. In order to achieve this success, local authorities have increasingly to rely on their capacity to generate and engage with complex networks of bargaining and negotiation with a broad range of local agencies.

Thus, analysis of change in both the organisation and management of local government and in its social and economic activities emphasises the increasingly central role being played by networks. The emerging pattern of governance at the local level is overwhelmingly *reticulate* in its form.

THE NATURE OF 'THE NETWORK'

The local governance network consists of a set of relationships of interdependency between the constituent organisations; these relationships may exist where organisations depend on each other for access to specific resources (for example, finance, skills, land), where there are functional interdependencies (so that organisations can only achieve their specific goals if other organisations do certain things), or where there is a mutual interest in tackling an issue which one organisation cannot deal with alone (for example, in complex issues such as urban deprivation). It is the growth in range and significance of these mutual dependencies between formally autonomous organisations that is one of the main characteristics of the process of change examined above.[12] Because they are founded on relations of interdependence, 'Networks will tend to be based upon concepts of reciprocity, rather than competition, and to require a degree of trust between the parties to the network'.[13] This points to the significance of networks as an alternative form of organisational system to the more familiar systems based on bureaucratic (hierarchical) relations or economic (market exchange) relations. It is the question of how this reticulated system operates in practice that is addressed in this section.

There are, however, two preliminary points to be made. First, although this collection is focusing on the appointed world of local governance, that is, the range of agencies that are in some sense part of the local state but separate from the democratically elected local authority, it can be artificial to focus solely on this if the concern is with the implications for the practice of local authorities. Relations between the local authority and the appointed agencies do not exist in a separate realm, they are – as has been argued in the previous section – themselves located in and influenced by a wider network which includes non-state agencies: the private sector and the voluntary sector. My focus is therefore on how local authorities are operating within the overall policy environment, but with particular reference to relations with the appointed agencies where appropriate.

Second, the interdependencies between organisations are not static, and nor do they necessarily lead to co-operation in practice. The relationships of the network are constantly changing as the constituent organisations seek both to minimise the possible negative consequences of dependency and to turn the recognition of common interests into mutual benefits. Whilst the principle of trust is fundamental to the successful operation of the network, it is a principle which itself has to be worked at in order to establish it in practice and to sustain it.

As suggested above, what actually goes on within the networks are processes of bargaining and negotiation, and the outcomes of these processes are themselves likely to affect the nature of the network. It is thus helpful to distinguish two levels of network operation. Bargaining and negotiation to identify areas of co-operation and conflict can be regarded as the first level of network practice. Here, essentially, organisations test each other out to assess the potential for building trust and for developing forms of collaboration; however, this process will sometimes reveal other interests or imperatives which override the recognition of interdependency leading to deadlock or hostile competition. Each organisation may then try to mobilise other parts of the network in order to outflank the competitor. But if these initial processes of negotiation are successful then a basis of trust and co-operation will be established and the second level of network operation, in which organisations develop means of working together towards positive outcomes, is achieved. It is on the nature of these sorts of 'second level' outcomes that I will concentrate in this section, rather than on the 'micro-processes' of negotiation that generate them.

Co-operative relationships between network organisations can be analysed using a simple three-fold typology which defines characteristics of both the *process* through which the relationship is expressed, and the *outcomes* of the process and their effects on the constituent organisations themselves and on the network. Defining and exemplifying each of the three types may also help in reducing some of the conceptual ambiguity that recent accounts of local policy networks have noted.[14]

Type 1: Alliances

Alliances are formed with the purpose of exerting influence and shaping opinion. They are characterised by a convergence of values between the co-operating organisations. The specific aim of the alliance will be to develop ways of acting together to influence outsiders to the network or to influence a third party within the network. Examples would be when the local authority and the Training and Enterprise Council (TEC) work together to influence policy change on training priorities on the part of central government, or to persuade local further education colleges to develop new courses to meet specific local needs.

Alliances seek to change organisational behaviour (including sometimes that of the allies themselves) but through indirect means; they leave existing organisational forms, including the form of the network, unchanged.

Type 2: Consortia

Consortia are concerned with establishing a joint approach to strategy and policy development and with joint decision making. They are characterised by a convergence of policy goals between the partners. Consortium aims will be defined in terms of the joint planning and co-ordination of specific projects or programmes, or of the use of collective resources in the most efficient and effective ways; or they may be defined in terms of the development of new forms of practice. Examples could include the local authority Social Services Department and the Health Authority developing a joint purchasing strategy for community health and social care services; or a consortium between the local education authority, the police and the probation services to develop a collaborative programme of crime prevention targeted at young people.

Consortia seek specific outcomes by tying the partners together in formal agreements to undertake joint action. The consortium will often have a specific identity as a task group, planning team or joint working party, but is not constituted as a separate organisational entity. It constitutes a new dimension to the network, since the collaborating organisations may now be represented in it both independently and, at times, jointly. The existing forms of the separate collaborating organisations themselves are, however, left unchanged.

Type 3: Partnerships

Partnerships are formed to ensure the implementation or delivery of specific objectives. They are characterised by a convergence of functional interest between the partner organisations. The aim of a partnership will be to create a new institutional capacity to achieve specific outcomes, in relation, for example, to a shared problem or need by establishing a distinct 'ownership' of that problem and directing specific resources to it. Examples of partnerships might include collaboration between the local authority and the Chamber of Commerce to create a separate organisation to promote and market the locality to prospective inward investors and visitors; and the establishment of a new careers service partnership by the local education authority and the TEC.

Partnerships pursue specific goals on behalf of their constituent bodies through a separate organisational form; they have an institutional independence from their progenitors, often established as companies limited by guarantee. They therefore imply change in the original organisations, because of the transfer of resources and functions to the new body, and to the network since they constitute a new and autonomous member of it.

Like all typologies, the one I have just sketched needs to be used with care and with recognition of its limitations. Not all of the forms of co-operative relationship that can emerge from local governance networks will slot easily into one of the three categories. Moreover, the typology does not do justice to the complexity of network relationships that exists in practice; it will often be the case, for instance, that two organisations are involved in different forms of co-operative relationship simultaneously. They may even be engaged at different *levels* of networking at the same time, involved in both co-operation and non-co-operation: unable to progress beyond deadlock in respect of one set of issues but establishing a positive outcome on another set.

In order to illustrate the potential complexity of local governance networks it will be helpful to consider an example of recent experience in Birmingham. The policy context is the government's announcement, in late 1993, of the new single regeneration budget (SRB – drawing together in one funding source a previously disparate range of grant regimes aimed at aspects of urban regeneration planned and delivered through local organisations) and the City Pride initiative, which invited local interests in Birmingham, Manchester and London to prepare a ten-year vision (or 'prospectus', in the government's language) for the future of their cities.[15] Bids for the SRB were to be co-ordinated jointly by the local authority and the TEC, while the development of the City Pride prospectus was to be led by the local authority but in close consultation with other major local interests.

The first, perhaps obvious, decision in Birmingham was that the SRB bid and the City Pride prospectus should be complementary: the SRB bid was 'framed within the context of the first City Pride Prospectus for Birmingham'.[16] The second key decision was that both documents would be prepared on behalf of, and in conjunction with, a wide range of local players. Some of these players are primary organisations in the local network, for instance the Chamber of Industry and Commerce and the Birmingham Voluntary Services Council, as well as other local statutory agencies – the health service, police and probation services and the further/higher education establishments. A further group consists of organisations which are themselves the product of earlier co-operation within the network but which have a formal status deriving from their financial and/or accountability relationship to central government. These are the 'local regeneration agencies' which in Birmingham include the Heartlands Urban Development Corporation, the Castle Vale Housing Action Trust, and the Newtown/South Aston City Challenge Company. Heartlands UDC has an interesting history, originating as an initiative of the city council and the local business community but eventually becoming a UDC in accordance with the partners' wishes. Uniquely, the UDC has substantial local authority representation on its board.[17] Likewise, the Housing Action Trust was actively lobbied for by an alliance of local authority, schools and colleges and the health authority, and the City Challenge Company was the result of an earlier collaborative bid.

Early efforts in response to the City Pride invitation, led by the city council, were directed at building alliances around the idea that a locally driven and systematic attempt to develop a common framework for shaping Birmingham's future was in the interest of all resident organisations. These efforts particularly focused on generating commitment to the principle that every sector of city life – business, statutory, voluntary, community – would have to be involved. Out of these preliminary discussions and negotiations, agreement was reached among sufficient allies that the best way of ensuring continuing high-level support for and ownership of the City Pride process and its outcomes would be to form a City Pride board, with senior representatives from all sectors.

The City Pride board can be regarded as a substantial consortium in terms of the above typology. Its terms of reference are to:

> Agree and commit to the vision and mission statement for City Pride; agree the parameters and key objectives of the City Pride prospectus, taking account of social and economic interests in Birmingham; present Birmingham's vision and case; agree the process of monitoring and evaluation of City Pride at a local level and influence monitoring and evaluation at national level; and formalise the partnership, representation process and commitment to City Pride.[18]

The board was established with, initially, 23 members, six of whom were Birmingham City councillors. It included representation from the UDC, HAT, and City Challenge Company, as well as from the more traditional statutory agencies, and business, voluntary and community groups. Professional and administrative support to the board is provided by an officer team drawn mainly from the city council but with assistance from named individuals from the Chamber, TEC, City 2000 (an organisation representing the financial and legal services sector) and the Voluntary Services Council. The board has overseen the production, and presentation to government, of Birmingham's City Pride prospectus and action plan and will provide continuing monitoring and evaluation throughout the period of the City Pride initiative.

The government's timescale meant that work on developing the SRB bid had to progress rather faster. The process was handled through a core consortium of the city council and the TEC, working with a number of other key agencies in various alliances to develop and finalise specific elements of the bid (which is a composite of five separate proposals linked to an overarching theme). A feature of the network associated with the SRB bid is the involvement of certain organisations that had been established through earlier local collaboration such as the Economic Development Partnership Limited (EDP) and the Birmingham Education Business Partnership Limited (BEBP).

Both the latter are good examples of the 'partnership' type of network organisation. The EDP's task is defined as co-ordination and integration of support to small and medium-sized businesses and business start-ups; it is also the parent company to a trading organisation, Birmingham Business Link, which offers advice and consultancy to businesses. The partners in the EDP are the city council, the Chamber, the TEC and the Department of Trade and Industry, with funds coming from TEC and city council programmes and contracts. The BEBP's remit is the co-ordination of all education/business partnership activities across the city, including teacher placement service, student work experience and education business compacts; the BEBP is itself the co-ordinating agency for ten local education business partnerships across the city. The partners are the Chamber, the LEA and the TEC, with the LEA and the TEC providing the budget. Both the EDP and the BEBP are seen as having major delivery (contractor) roles in relation to SRB bid objectives.

The City Pride prospectus and the SRB bid both envisage the creation of a range of new consortia and partnerships in order to deliver various objectives. Two examples (deliberately chosen from outside the conventional economic development arena) are:

1. Development of a 'University of the First Age', aiming to extend educational choice for young people in the city by complementing school provision, providing interest-led courses with qualifications and using multi-media and information technology learning systems; this requires a new partnership involving major telecommunications companies, the local authority, the Open University and the three existing universities in Birmingham.
2. A consortium of housing providers and housing financers to develop a model for understanding and shaping the housing market in Birmingham, maximising the local resources of finance, land and expertise, and widening the range of available housing in the city.

This highly abbreviated description of the network that mobilised in Birmingham in response to one national policy initiative illustrates a number of points. First, returning to the theme of the first section, it provides one example of how local government is responding to the challenges and opportunities presented by macro-processes of socio-economic change. It suggests a deliberate, local authority-led convergence of policy domains and institutional interests around a new agenda of city-based economic and social regeneration: an indication of the possibility of a locally driven *re-integration* of policies and resources from the remnants of nationally driven *fragmentation*, via an urban politics firmly grounded in local networks.[19] (It does not, of course, address the question of whether this new agenda can succeed, given the growing gap between urban needs and the public resources made available to meet them.)

Second, it shows the distinctions between the different organisational forms that network relationships adopt and gives some indication of the interplay between them: alliances, consortia and partnerships are all identifiable both as elements of the network process and as products of the network. Third, it suggests that complex inter-agency networks are increasingly being seen by local government not just as an unfortunate and unwelcome addition to the environment in which they operate – and as a symptom of their own loss of local power – but as resources which can be used to the benefit of local areas and which can provide the local authority itself with a new kind of empowerment through network coordination and leadership.

The account therefore reveals the extent to which operating within networks is central to the local authority's strategy process in complex policy areas such as urban regeneration. It is to a brief concluding overview of the implications for the policy process in local government of this approach to networks that I now turn.

IMPLICATIONS FOR THE LOCAL AUTHORITY POLICY PROCESS

Operating within networks is not, of course, a new experience for local government. However, the active, positive and often catalytic role now being played by local authorities in the development of alliances, consortia and partnerships with appointed agencies and business organisations suggests considerable implications for the existing internal management systems of authorities.[20] In particular, the growing importance of networks as the vehicles through which many of an authority's strategic aims must be realised points to a new kind of policy decision-making process within the authority. Whilst detailed specification of this new process cannot be attempted here, a number of propositions about some of its likely characteristics can be advanced:

- the internal policy process will much less concerned with the direct application of power in order to achieve desired policy outcomes than has traditionally been the case
- the formulation of the local authority's policy objectives – the desired policy outcomes – will itself be shaped in the process of dialogue and negotiation with other agencies
- the local authority will need 'a strong sense of its own identity, in terms of strategic direction and organizational priorities'[21] if it is to fulfil its potential role as leader of the local network and to be able to negotiate effectively

- the authority will need specific organisational capacities, especially the capacity to 'read' the local networks and to assess when and how they can best be used (and when other means of achieving objectives should be explored)
- the local authority will still have the unique advantage of democratic legitimacy, giving it a status and a resource that constitute powerful bargaining chips in dealing with other organisations in the local governance network and a specific responsibility to ensure the public accountability of the network
- the role of elected councillors as policy makers will be geared towards the exercise of influence using the authority's 'authority' as the organisation of governance which represents the locality
- the role of senior officers in policy making will be concerned with managing the interface between the authority and the local governance network, emphasising skills of negotiation, brokerage and fixing in inter-organisational relations
- the institutional context of policy making will shift from one of organisational management to one of network management.

Many of these characteristics of a new approach to policy making in local government are already discernible, but it is also true that currently they exist uneasily within organisational structures and cultures that were created to serve the needs of local authorities operating in a far less interdependent institutional environment. Thus, local authorities retain a decision-making process based on a structure of individual service committees, which by its nature is not well placed to engage strategically with the holistic and flexible functioning of policy networks. The division now frequently found between 'client' committees and 'provider' committees, whilst seeming to denote a more outward-looking approach on the part of the client, still serves to emphasise specific service responsibilities rather than overarching needs and opportunities; indeed the separation can restrain the learning and the adaptability that are required to respond effectively to fast changing local needs.[22] On the other hand, in many authorities, the central policy and resources committee (or similar) is increasingly geared towards explicit management of the authority's position within various networks. Such committees, assisted by new sub-committees focusing on different aspects of inter-agency relations and, sometimes, by new forms of corporate chief officer support, provide the formal arena in which the authority's policy relationship to the outside world is defined and in which a more holistic view of the authority's strategic choices can be taken.

However, this effort is hampered not only by the power of the service committees within the authority (whose individual interests frequently clash with the corporate concerns of the central committee), but by difficulties in establishing effective means of ensuring that councillors who are involved in working with other parts of the network are adequately briefed on the authority's strategic interests and are in turn keeping their colleagues fully informed. So far, the organisational processes required to ensure coherence and consistency within a more diversified pattern of involvement with local policy initiatives are inadequately developed. The danger is of individual councillors (and officers) developing a strong entrepreneurial role in relation to other local agencies in the absence of strong institutional links back into the local authority. The development of policy and strategy then becomes divorced from the democratic institution which gives it both power and legitimacy.

CONCLUSION

Working within the new networks of local governance has become increasingly significant for local authorities as they seek to respond both to substantial changes in their own capacity for action and to changing relationships between localities, national government and global social and economic forces. New types of organisation, based on co-operative relationships between formally autonomous agencies, are emerging to play an important part in the development and implementation of local policies. Local authorities are frequently taking the lead in the creation of local alliances, consortia and partnerships across the public, private and community sectors; and there is at least some justification for an optimistic view that it is in such activities that the potential for a reassertion of the necessity of strong local democratic government can be realised. Such a trend does, however, pose a major challenge for local authorities to the extent that it implies a new and different approach to their own internal policy processes. Whether local authorities can respond by transforming their internal roles and relationships to support their changing role in the external environment may be a critical factor in determining whether they can consolidate and enhance their position as the leaders of local networks or whether they will be relegated to a role of camp followers.

NOTES

1. For a helpful review of the burgeoning literature on this issue, see A. Amin, 'Post-Fordism: Models, Fantasies and Phantoms of Transition', in A. Amin (ed.), *Post-Fordism: A Reader* (Oxford, 1994), pp.1–39.
2. G. Stoker, 'Regulation Theory, Local Government and the Transition from Fordism', in D.S. King and J. Pierre (eds.), *Challenges to Local Government* (London, 1990), pp.242–64.
3. D. Prior, J. Stewart and K. Walsh, *Citizenship. Rights, Community and Participation*

(London, 1995), pp.15–16.

4. N. Flynn, *Public Sector Management* (Hemel Hempstead, 1993); J. Newman and J. Clarke, 'Going about Our Business? The Managerialization of Public Services', in J. Clarke, A. Cochrane and E. McLaughlin (eds.), *Managing Social Policy* (London, 1994), pp.13–31.

5. J. Stewart and G. Stoker, 'Fifteen Years of Local Government Restructuring 1979–1994: An Evaluation', in J. Stewart and G. Stoker (eds.), *Local Government in the 1990s* (London, 1995), p.197.

6. K. Walsh, 'Competition and Public Service Delivery', in Stewart and Stoker, op. cit., pp.28–48.

7. B. Jessop, 'Post-Fordism and the State', in Amin, op. cit., pp.271–3.

8. M. Mayer, 'Post-Fordist City Politics', in Amin, op. cit., p.319.

9. A. Amin and N. Thrift, 'Globalization, Institutional "Thickness" and the Local Economy', in P. Healey, S. Cameron, S. Davoudi, S. Graham and A. Madani-Pour (eds.), *Managing Cities* (Chichester, 1995); D.S. King, 'Economic Activity', in King and Pierre, op. cit., pp.279–84.

10. Jessop, op. cit., p.272.

11. Mayer, op.cit., p.319.

12. S. Leach, J. Stewart and K. Walsh, *The Changing Organisation and Management of Local Government* (London, 1994), pp.63–8.

13. Ibid., p.66.

14. M. Mackintosh, 'Partnership: Issues of Policy and Negotiation', *Local Economy*, Vol.7, No.3 (1992), pp.210–24; N. Deakin and J. Edwards, *The Enterprise Culture and the Inner City* (London, 1993), pp.9–13; V. Roberts, H. Russell, A. Harding and M. Parkinson, *Public/Private/Voluntary Partnerships in Local Government. Report to the Local Government Management Board* (Liverpool, 1994), pp.5–7.

15. For a fuller account of the policy context and implications of these developments, see: P. Le Gales and J. Mawson, 'Contracts versus Competitive Bidding: Rationalizing Urban Policy Programmes in England and France', *Journal of European Public Policy*, Vol.2, No.2 (1995), pp.205–41.

16. Birmingham City Council and Birmingham Training and Enterprise Council, *Birmingham Single Regeneration Budget Bid 1995–2000* (Birmingham, n/d).

17. A detailed account of the development of the Heartlands initiative to a point just before it became a UDC is provided by Deakin and Edwards, op. cit., pp.130–63.

18. Birmingham City Pride, *Appendices* (Birmingham, 1994), Appendix Q.

19. Le Gales and Mawson, op. cit., p.201

20. Leach, Stewart and Walsh, op. cit., p.63.

21. Ibid., p.87.

22. Stewart and Stoker, op. cit. p.201.